THE BEGINNER'S GUIDE TO THE GOSPEL MUSIC INDUSTRY

A Handbook For Aspiring Artists and Industry Executives

MONICA A. COATES

PAUL MARCHELL
PUBLISHING

Paul Marchell Publishing
P.O. Box 682854
Franklin, TN 37068
Orders: *pmpublishing@monicacoates.com* or *www.monicacoates.com*

Unattributed quotations are by Monica Coates.

Unless otherwise indicated, all Scripture quotations are taken from the King James Version of the Bible.

Scripture quotations marked NIV are taken from the HOLY BIBLE, NEW INTERNATIONAL VERSION®. Copyright © 1973, 1978, 1984 International Bible Society. Used by permission of Zondervan. All rights reserved.

The "NIV" and "New International Version" trademarks are registered in the United States Patent and Trademark Office by International Bible Society. Use of either trademark requires the permission of International Bible Society.

Library of Congress Control Number
2009901495

ISBN: 978-0-9823600-0-2

IMPORTANT NOTE—DISCLAIMER

The materials in this book represent the opinions of the author and may not be applicable to every situation. Accordingly, the author and publisher assume no responsibility for actions taken by readers based upon the advice offered in this book. Each reader should use caution when applying the information in this book to his or her specific situation, and as needed, seek the advice of an appropriate professional.

Every effort has been made to ensure the accuracy of the materials in this book. However, some changes may have occurred in policy, law, or custom during the lapse between the writing and printing of this book.

The music industry is not an exact science and is constantly changing. Therefore, we recommend each reader be both wise and prayerful.

For P. Anthony and Camille,
whose lives continue to inspire me.

Acknowledgments

For my entire life as a Gospel music consumer, I have had an unnatural excitement about reading the liner notes for an album. Thank yous brought me a special joy—until I had to write them. I finally understand why every artist who has ever had to deliver album copy to me saved the thank yous for last, relinquishing them to me begrudgingly and with great hesitation. So, to every artist on whom I have cracked the whip over getting their thank yous in, I offer my deepest, most heart-felt apologies!

I wish to express my sincere thanks to:

My immediate family—Doris E., Eric L. Coates, and Felicia Coates. Although our numbers seem small, our strength and faith are great. The legacy is long and growing. Thank you for your constant prayers, support, and love. You have given me more than I will ever be able to give to you. To my extended family, the Coates and Elam families, I love and appreciate you all so much.

To my readers—Ken Pennell, Beau Black, Joann Rosario, Manny & Shannon Saiz, Erik & Janice Gaines. Your insight and suggestions improved this work immensely.

It would be difficult for me to name all of the artists whom I have had the pleasure to serve over the years. I hesitate to try because I know I will leave someone out. Please know that my time with you was treasured, even in moments of crisis. I consider it an honor to have served beside and with you. I must mention the following artists whose presence in my life had the biggest impact on me personally: Fred Hammond, Joann Rosario, Pastor Donnie McClurkin, Donald Lawrence, and Bishop Hezekiah Walker.

I never understood the value of a pastor until I had a truly great one. Thank you to Pastors Reginald & Kelly Lane and to Apostle Nahum & Pastora Minerva Rosario. Your wisdom, prayers, challenges, and lives of integrity shaped and matured me in ways I will never be able to repay.

To my friends in this industry who have brightened my days, listened to my tears, prayed with and challenged me. Thank you for giving me a reason to show up at the office, in the studio, or on the road even on the hardest days. This is not nearly an exhaustive list, but I have to acknowledge Kevin Wilson and PamKenyon Donald, Damon Williams, Jojo Pada, Dalia Glickman, Jessica Castro, Damon Ellis, Karen Scott Jackson, Erin Barlow-Haggerty, Ta'mar Poole, Darwin & Traci Hobbs, Asaph Ward, Aaron & Adrian Lindsey, Tiffany Palmer-Bastiany, Danielle Stephens, Fred Purifoy, Terrell Carter, Tiffany Smith, Resa Bell, Roudy Michel, Carla Williams, Cheryl Moore, Nancy Roof, Gabrielle Rosen, Gaby Ruiz, and Jerard & Jovaun Woods.

To the many industry associates who have opened doors and made my jobs easier over the years, especially Max Siegel and Jazzy Jordan.

To Bill Hearn, Ken Pennell, and the people of EMI CMG, who taught me how to merge a life of faith with a commitment to professionalism.

I have been blessed to have long-term friendships with some amazing people. Special thanks to Lisa & Wesley Wyatt, Lauri

Johnson, Ainisha Persaud, Tiffany Byrd, Ed & Tina Green, David & Celeste Ivey, Stacey & Rozelle White, and John Taylor. Your advice, support, and prayers during this season were invaluable.

To Mark Luckey for always pushing me and supporting me with your wealth of skills, talents, and gadgets. You and Shonna will always be family to me.

A big thank you to Micha Berman, who generously shared his knowledge and set the bar high.

To Judith Paterson (University of Maryland, Philip Merrill College Of Journalism), who first encouraged me to pursue non-fiction writing. Also to Melvin Butler (University of Virginia), who gave me a forum to share my knowledge. My teaching notes for your class became the foundation for this book.

To all of the artists, producers, and songwriters who have ever trusted me to listen to the fruit of their hearts, I thank you. Your openness and courage have helped me to grow in my own gifts and talents.

To Marshall Grant (Grantmx Enterprises, LLC), Michele DeFilippo, Ronda Rawlins (1106 Design), and Lynda Bonfante. Thank you for transforming my ideas into a physical reality.

To those who took an early interest in this work, opening their hearts and extending their resources, particularly E.J. at Gospelpundit.com, Gerard Henry at you129.com, Jojo at Ignition PR, and Terry Woods at Central South Distribution.

Finally, I extend my very special thanks to Joann Rosario and the Rosario family for giving me a safe place to heal so that the Holy Spirit could produce this work. Your generosity and love will never be forgotten.

Contents

Introduction **1**
Calling Versus Gifts And Talents 3

Part One: The Basics **9**
The Three Sectors Of The Gospel Music Industry 11
The Creative Community (ARTISTRY) 15
The Business Community (INDUSTRY) 19
The Church Community (MINISTRY) 27

Part Two: For The Aspiring Artist **33**
The Call To Artistry 35
Necessary Elements 37
First Steps 69
The Value Of A Record Deal 91

Part Three: For The Aspiring Industry Executive **111**
The Call To Industry 113
My Story (The Beginning) 117
Roles Within The Business Community 131
First Steps 141
The Value Of Excellence 157

Part Four: Changing Times   175

A Brief Overview   177
The End Of The Specialty Music Retailer   181
The Impact Of The Megaretailers   183
Developing Artists Feel The Pinch   185
Now What?   189

Index   193

Introduction

IF YOU'RE READING THESE WORDS right now, it is a safe bet that
you are an aspiring artist, musician, or music industry professional. Whatever your area of interest, please allow me to welcome
you to the Gospel music industry.

I honestly believe the pursuit of a career in the Gospel music
industry can be one of the most interesting, exciting, and educational experiences you will ever undertake. But I must also caution
you that it will be challenging, often frustrating, and—if you are
serious about ministry as well—it will test you in ways you weren't
exactly expecting. Nevertheless, be encouraged!

This handbook, when read in its entirety and put to proper
use, will help you avoid many tragic mistakes. Even better, it will
assist you in turning unavoidable mistakes into pivotal moments
from which you will mature and grow.

My desire is to help you to walk beyond the threshold of gifts and talents at which you presently stand into a world where those gifts and talents can be properly nurtured to assist you in fulfilling your calling.

And, believe it or not, that's an excellent place for us to start.

Calling Versus Gifts And Talents

It would be difficult for me to begin any honest discussion of the basics of the Gospel music industry without first discussing the concept of calling versus gifts and talents.

I firmly believe we each have an assignment from God for which our gifts and talents are merely tools. God, in His infinite wisdom and love, designed us with an overall purpose in mind—a long-term goal. I like to call that long-term goal our **calling**.

To accomplish that calling, I believe God has given each of us a treasure chest of abilities that will inform, assist, and provide for us along the way. Those abilities often begin as seeds, and over time, become apparent to us as our unique **gifts and talents**.

Our challenge is two-fold. First we must discover the long-term goal God has for us—our calling. Secondly, and often more importantly, we must learn to distinguish that calling from our gifts and talents—the **tools**—intended to act as support for us on our journey.

In my experience, this concept is rarely discussed when people are thinking about making a career in Gospel music. Yet for us, I believe this concept is particularly vital.

The ultimate result of our efforts should be to spread the message and love of Jesus Christ through the musical products we create, promote, broadcast, and sell. With such an important mission at stake, it is crucial for us to be sure we are pursuing our true calling rather than spending years of heartfelt effort focusing our energies to develop a tool beyond its intended function.

Here's an example of that principle: I come from a musical family. Almost all of my mother's family sings or plays an instrument, and because my father held a great love for music as well, my two siblings and I were encouraged to learn at least one instrument of our own. We all took piano lessons and when the time came to pursue instrumental music in junior high school, we were each given an instrument.

My sister and brother went on to pursue voice lessons and both became highly celebrated in high school competition and in college at the national level. And I—easily the least musically talented of the three—continued to study instrumental music through high school and to sing in various choirs along with playing piano through college.

Combine that rich musical environment with a musical church world and a powerful love for recorded Gospel music, and people would naturally assume that when I began to pursue a career in the Gospel industry, I would have been a musician or singer.

I must admit in the earliest days of my music industry career, in the back of my mind, as I was meeting world-class Gospel musicians and singers, I hoped to perhaps increase my musical skills. And occasionally I would daydream of that moment of perfect performance on a national stage.

Fortunately for me, the Lord showed me very early in my career that was *not* His long-term goal for me. As I sought Him in a season of prayer during my last year in graduate school, He revealed to me a calling of service to the Gospel music industry.

From the beginning, during my unpaid, entry-level days, it was clear to see that while my musical skills and gifts gave me a wonderful background and point of identification with the companies and artists I served, those musical gifts were *not* my calling.

And in later years, as bigger doors began to open at executive levels in the industry, my creative background became an important well of information from which I could draw on a daily basis. Nearly every skill needed for my various music industry jobs—from hearing the potential in a demo, to predicting a radio hit, to understanding the difference between a good mix and a bad mix on a song—had its root in my musical background.

My gifts and talents provided for me a strong set of tools to use in my career. And as I continued to develop those tools, I gained new professional opportunities.

Clearly my musical gifts were a blessing from the Lord and something He intended for me to value and nurture. However, had I pursued those gifts as if they were my calling, it is doubtful I would have ever been successful on a national level.

Understanding God's long-term goal for me put me in the position where I was able to identify and accept opportunities beyond my dreams. And as an unanticipated benefit, it freed me from any potential struggle with the notion of my own stardom. I was confident in the value of my role because my mission was clear to me. My gifts and talents were the tools that enabled me to fulfill my calling—serving my artists and my industry.

I have come to believe any artist, musician, or industry professional aspiring toward a career in Gospel must deal early and honestly with this issue of calling.

Yet I fully understand why many of us would prefer not to examine this too closely. It is scary to risk your dream by asking God the difficult question, "What have you created me to do?"

That was one of the hardest steps I had to make in my walk with the Lord. What if the things that were the most important to me proved to be unimportant to Him?

The question is challenging, but we must never forget the kind of God we serve. God is *for* us.

During the time in my life when I was asking that question for the first time, the Lord showed me this scripture:

> *"For I know the plans I have for you," declares the LORD, "plans to prosper you and not to harm you, plans to give you hope and a future." (Jeremiah 29:11, NIV)*

In all my years of church and personal Bible reading, it was the first time I ever saw that scripture. God's timing couldn't have been more perfect! At one of the scariest moments in my life, He took the time to assure me that His heart is toward me. God is *for* me.

Please know His heart is the same toward you. He has a plan for you. He has a long-term goal in mind and He has already given you the tools you need to accomplish that goal.

Before we move on, please take a moment and ask Him, "What have you created me to do?" Then please listen with an open heart.

I have provided some space for you to record your thoughts and any words the Lord might speak to you at this time.

Thoughts and Notes

Part One:
The Basics

The Three Sectors Of The
Gospel Music Industry

Long before I imagined a career in the Gospel music industry, I was a devoted fan of the music. It may actually be an understatement to use the word fan to describe myself at that time. I loved the music, I loved the artists and I would spend hours after purchasing a new album reading every word on the packaging—LP sleeves, then cassette tray cards, then CD booklets.

From the time I was a pre-teen, I could tell you the name of the studio in which Andraé Crouch tended to record his songs and which musicians were a regular part of his team. I could tell you who wrote the liner notes on the back of Walter Hawkins' *Love Alive* album. I could even tell you the city and state in which the major Gospel record companies were located.

(It is obvious that from the beginning, God gave me the gifts and talents to do exactly what I'm doing!)

Yet with all of the time spent listening to Gospel music, reading Christian music magazines, and hanging out in the music section of my favorite Christian bookstores, I knew very little about the structure of Gospel music as an industry.

Surprisingly, many years later when I was blessed to actually work in Gospel music, I found there was virtually no concise and easily understood information on how the Gospel music industry functioned as a business.

I was extremely blessed to work with people early in my career who insisted I spend a lot of time listening and watching the industry world around me, rather than asserting my own opinions.

In fact, one of the best pieces of advice I ever received came from one of my mentors, Fred Hammond. The week before I officially reported for duty as his assistant—my first job in Gospel music—he said very simply, "Listen more than you speak."

I heard those words as if they were the voice of the Holy Spirit. And in the years since, I have become convinced that they were. The compulsion to share whatever limited intellect I had at the time was put on a shelf. Instead, I did my very best to watch and listen to the professionals around me respectfully, attentively, avidly. I learned to be an active listener, applying each new term and phrase to the bits of information I already had in my head from those years of reading liner notes. And slowly the Gospel music industry began to make sense to me.

Although the music world around us is changing every day, I believe it is terribly important for any aspiring artist, musician, or industry professional to know certain basics about the structure of this industry. Without a foundational concept of the world you are preparing to enter, it is easy to make costly errors by moving blindly, using precious resources improperly, and offending experienced professionals who might otherwise be inclined to offer you useful information.

So let's begin.

There are three basic sectors to the Gospel Music industry:

- The Creative Community (**artistry**)
- The Business Community (**industry**)
- The Church Community (**ministry**)

In many ways, each of these sectors is a world of its own, rich with unique personalities and protocols. Within the commercial world of Gospel music, these communities overlap in ways that are often complex, but extremely important to understand in order to be successful. The first two communities closely mirror the mainstream (secular) music industry. The third community is unique to Gospel music and requires certain spiritual considerations, which anyone aspiring to this marketplace should not attempt to avoid.

The Creative Community (ARTISTRY)

The first and easily the most recognizable sector of the music industry is the creative community, the artistry. Regardless of the genre of music, most of the public is familiar with this sector. In fact, if truth be told, most people believe the artistry is all there is to the music industry.

Almost any churchgoer anywhere in our nation could tell you who Fred Hammond, Donnie McClurkin, Yolanda Adams, and Kirk Franklin are. We sing their songs, but we also know their faces, watch them on TV, and attend their concerts.

The creative community—the artistry—primarily consists of the following:

- Artists (the people who perform the music)
- Songwriters (the people who write the music)
- Producers (the people who develop the songs into recorded music)

These people are the driving force in the industry. They create the product. They **are** the product. Without our creative community, we would have no songs, no CDs, no concerts, no ministry.

The creative community is the primary reason for the existence of the music industry. In a very real sense, without people with the drive to create and perform, the rest of us wouldn't have jobs. Truly, the industry that has developed over the years to promote and sell music is multi-layered and complex, but it will always be the artists who are out front, performing, sharing themselves, touching people, and hopefully changing lives.

Because artists have such high visibility, most people who aspire to work in the music industry are eager to break into this first sector. For every one aspiring industry executive I have ever met, I have easily met fifty aspiring artists.

If you turn on your TV the second or third week of January each year, you will see further proof of that phenomenon. Every year all across the United States, people will come by the thousands, braving the elements to stand in line for hours for a chance to sing one minute of the song of their choosing before a panel of highly recognizable—and often brutally honest—judges with the hope of becoming a star.

I have to admire the courage it takes to walk out such a passionate dream in front of a national audience. Nevertheless, I must admit it breaks my heart as well. Those shows, by emphasizing stardom over artistry, tend to display a music world that is 100% based upon talent. The ability to sing is the thing, and if you have a good enough voice and a workable style, in less than a year, you could become one of the most recognizable faces and names in the world.

No one can deny that outlets like these, for many people, offer a once-in-a-lifetime chance to catch their big break. However, getting a big break without having a concept of the demands of the music industry is often a recipe for disaster; and to be launched into a career, without any understanding of the lifestyle of an artist, can have devastating effects on a person's mind, body, spirit, and creativity.

Lately, I've seen more than enough evidence of this in the news and on the Internet, as one reality contest winner after another finds himself or herself without a record deal, dropping out of concert tours, or failing under the pressure of celebrity.

I have also noticed that those who seem to avoid failure often either possessed more artistic experience from the beginning or continued to work to develop their creative and professional skills once the reality show was over.

Contrary to what most of America sees, for recording artists, sustained success on a national level is more like 30% talent and 70% dedication, hard work, sacrifice and, specialized knowledge in a variety of areas. Those areas would include the following:

- Developing a unique sound
- Communicating with an audience
- Putting together a show
- Developing a ministry focus
- Building a relationship with a record company
- Building an effective management team

I'm afraid the list could go on for quite some time.

I can honestly say many of the nationally known Gospel artists who I have had the pleasure to know are particularly skilled at most of those areas. In just a few moments in conversation with them about their craft, listening to them live in concert or sitting in one of their studio sessions, it becomes clear that while their talent is memorable, it is their mastery of the other elements that truly makes them legendary.

It is important to note that Gospel artists have a dual challenge in their careers, which their mainstream counterparts do not share. As we will see shortly, because the Church Community plays such a vital role in the Gospel music industry, Gospel artists must master the skill of ministry as well as mastering the music industry world.

Gospel audiences don't just expect a good album or a great show. They also expect a message that will aid them in their lives and an experience that will enhance their relationships with God.

To meet that challenge, it is extremely important for Gospel artists to spend time developing their spiritual lives as well as their creative skills. There must be ample time spent on building a relationship with God and accountability to a local church. And special attention should be paid to learning to live and work with integrity.

The key is this: Your talent may get you in the door, but your ability to master the demands of the industry, along with the demands of ministry, will determine your success and longevity.

With all of those things in mind, it may be a bit easier now to see why our gifts and talents must not be the primary focus. Our talent by itself will never be enough to sustain us. But when we are sure of our calling, when we are in line with God's long-term goal for us, we have confidence that our God-given gifts and talents will be the necessary tools to accomplish that calling.

If you are an aspiring member of the creative community, take a moment and breathe. Resist the urge to become overwhelmed. We've just begun and I believe help is on the way!

For now, let's move on to the second sector.

The Business Community (INDUSTRY)

A few pages ago, I mentioned that most churchgoers in our nation would easily recognize the names of our top Gospel artists. It would be much harder to find a churchgoer who would recognize names like Bill Hearn, Ken Pennell, Shiba Freeman, Roger Holmes, Al Wash, or Larry Robinson. Yet without those people, many of our favorite artists might never have achieved the national prominence they currently have and certainly deserve.

The people I just named are highly successful in the second sector of the music industry, the Business Community. These are the business owners, executives, and employees who maintain and advance the complex commercial structure that has grown up around the creative community.

To be more specific, the business community consists of all of the following:

- Record companies
- Managers/Booking Agents
- Radio
- Media (TV, print, Internet)
- Promoters (live performances)
- Retail (sales outlets)

This community of people provides the structure for the music marketplace. They are the link between art and commerce. They fund the music, market the music, and sell the music.

Ironically, while the Business Community is the largest sector of the music industry, it is also the least visible, least understood part of the industry. A vast majority of people in the general public, as well as many within the Creative Community, don't truly understand the industry and how it operates.

The business of the music industry can be extremely complicated. Nevertheless, I believe we can begin to develop a working knowledge by first looking at the basic relationship between these first two sectors of the music industry.

Historically, the Business and Creative Communities have interacted in this basic way:

Record companies discover an artist and, together with that artist's **management team**, develop the artist's career by providing the money and guidance for creating albums, establishing that artist's image (look, style, and public persona), and presenting that artist to retail.

In order for an album to have a genuine shot at commercial success, a record company must attempt to connect the artist and his or her music to the general public. The more powerfully a record company makes that connection, the more successful an artist and an album will become.

How exactly is such a connection made?

Simply stated, record companies make the connection between an album or artist and the public by utilizing their relationships with radio stations and media to inform the public that a new artist or new project is on the way.

The promotion department of a record company will pick a key song (a single) from the project to send to **radio** stations across the country with the intention that radio program directors and announcers will play the song frequently enough for people to begin to recognize it and look for the CD.

Likewise, the publicity department of a record company will create materials—normally photos, a biography, and press kit—to send to members of the **media** (newspaper and magazine editors) throughout the country with the intention of getting articles written about the artist and new CD. The publicist will also send those materials to television producers at high-profile shows, hoping to gain on-air appearances for that artist to perform and/or talk about the new CD.

In addition to these efforts, the management team and **booking agent** for an artist will attempt to secure promotional (unpaid) and paid opportunities for the artist to perform the music before a live audience. These events may either be individual performances or a highly structured series of concerts (a tour) in connection with a concert **promoter.**

All of those efforts working together should create a significant impression on potential consumers across the country. The sales department at the record company can now use that "buzz" to convince buyers at **retail** outlets across the country to purchase the CD from the record company and keep it in stock in their various locations.

The more successfully the parts of the system work, the higher an artist's profile becomes, and the more copies of the CD will be sold.

Now you understand why a particular artist seems to be everywhere, singing the same song in the weeks before his or her new CD hits the stores! It is the result of a highly coordinated effort on the part of key members of the business community.

When I first began working in this marketplace, I had no idea any of that was happening. But the more I watched and listened, the more I began to see how complex and deliberate the process was. I also began to understand that there were wonderful opportunities for someone with my skill set to be of service in such an environment.

For example, interacting with the media by writing press releases, creating press kits, and devising media campaigns were skills I had studied while pursuing my master's degree in journalism. Back then, my primary intention was to be a writer. However, as the Lord began to reveal the bits and pieces of His long-term goal for me, I started looking for ways to diversify my education accordingly. I met with my advisors and added public relations classes to my planned curriculum.

It was an act of faith based upon what I was hearing in my prayer time. But as I took the first steps to find out more, God began to show me how well He had already ordered my steps.

Let me explain:

Most people are probably not aware that the public relations divisions of many universities are housed within their journalism and communications departments. I had already completed a year in the graduate journalism school of the University of Maryland before I was fully aware of that fact.

Subsequently, when I met with my advisor to discuss my new interest, he was able to show me very easily how I could amend my planned program to add the additional classes *without delay in completing my degree.* Amazing! The Lord confirmed that as I trusted in Him, He truly was directing my path (Proverbs 3:5–6).

It is important for me to point out that while God had provided me with all of the information and assistance I needed, the responsibility was upon me to seek Him first and then to be obedient in taking small steps toward His will for me.

I must also tell you, it wasn't until my sixth year in this marketplace that I would actually be in a position to use those particular public relations skills to further the cause of Gospel music. Nevertheless, God's ways are perfect.

When I stumbled upon the job of Director, Media and Promotion at EMI Gospel in 1998, I had already gained enough knowledge of the Gospel industry overall to add real substance to my skill set. Because God delayed my PR career, I came to that job with more than a working knowledge of the Gospel industry.

I truly believe that fact enabled me to be of far greater value to my artists and my company. Instead of coming to the job with a sterile, textbook approach to public relations, I arrived in Nashville with six years of hardcore Gospel music industry experience. I understood the implications of the media relationships I would form and the press releases I would write. I valued the hearts and concerns of my artists enough to bring both passion and compassion to my work on their behalf. Perhaps most importantly, I understood the impact my work ethic would have, not only on the careers and ministries of my artists, but on their daily lives as well.

I wanted to share that part of my story here because I believe it points to the significance of the relationship between the Business Community and the Creative Community. Perhaps because I began my career working directly with an artist, I developed my business skills surrounded by daily reminders of the ways in which my efforts could enhance or hinder the efforts of my partners in the Creative Community.

It can be quite challenging for industry workers and artists to understand and value each other's roles partly because the sectors of the industry differ so greatly from each other. Furthermore, the needs and goals of big business can often be in conflict with the needs and goals of artistry.

On the best day under the best circumstances, the music industry will always be a collective of uneasy alliances. Nevertheless, I believe it is important to view the relationships between the sectors as *necessary* alliances. Our thinking and systems may evolve to meet the needs of a changing music economy, but artistry will always require some form of industry.

Now you have a very general idea of how the parts work together. For the purposes of our discussion, I've kept the process simple. In reality, each step I've described requires a great deal of specialized knowledge and often involves several key players.

With that in mind, it is easy to understand why members of the creative community are often uncomfortable with the music industry. If your primary goal is to make and perform music that you love, the notion of having to learn to negotiate your way through so complex a world can seem unnecessary and even scary.

As a result, many aspiring artists choose to focus solely on the creative process and never take the time to learn about the other parts of the music industry. That is a mistake.

Countless times, I have taken phone calls or had meetings with aspiring artists, musicians, producers, and songwriters who have reached out to me for assistance and advice on some area of their careers. I have listened and often I have been able to offer concrete, basic instruction for what steps can be taken to accomplish their goals.

Too often, they fail to follow up on that advice, and inevitably, I will receive an urgent and sometimes tearful phone call several months later from those same dear people.

I do not say that to boast regarding my own advice. I consider it a blessing to be able to give counsel or guidance to a creative friend in need. But I do believe it's important for us to challenge ourselves to invest as much time and energy into becoming excellent professionals as we are willing to invest into becoming excellent artists.

No matter where the future of the music industry takes us, in order to maintain a career in Gospel music, artists will always have to be knowledgeable about industry and willing to form alliances with members of the Business Community. It is one of the methods God has given us to earn a living from our calling.

One final note: A few pages ago I said, **"Historically**, the Business and Creative communities have interacted" in the way I described. Our marketplace is changing drastically—and daily. Consequently, many of the roles I briefly outlined have shifted in response to those changes. Furthermore, in the advent of the digital age, changes in the way the general public acquires and uses music have resulted in dramatic shifts that we are just beginning to understand.

Regardless of those facts, I believe it is important to develop a concept of how the pieces have fit together for the majority of music industry history. Without an understanding of the past, it becomes very difficult to understand both our present and our future.

The Church Community (MINISTRY)

While the mainstream music industry has both a Creative Community and a Business Community, the third sector we will discuss, the Church Community, is unique to the genre of Gospel music.

Quite simply, the Church Community consists of churches on a local, national, and international level. Structurally, this community is not directly connected to the music industry. However, functionally, the Church Community impacts almost every aspect of the Gospel music industry. Consider these points:

- Virtually every known Gospel artist began singing and developing their talent in the local church.
- The content and style of Gospel songs is based upon, and often inspired by, spiritual concepts and musical styles introduced in church services.
- The product of the Gospel music industry—Gospel music—is often the primary content of church worship services.
- Gospel artists make their primary living from performances in or connected to churches.

In just these brief ways, it quickly becomes clear that the Church Community is often the **source** for talent, the **inspiration** for the music, the **showcase** for Gospel music product, and the **primary forum** for Gospel artists. Functionally speaking, therefore, it would be quite difficult to have a successful Gospel music industry without the Church Community.

Because the church plays such a vital role in the Gospel music industry, a basic acceptance of the fundamental concepts of Christianity and a working knowledge of ministry issues are essential for anyone who would make a career here. For this reason, I believe it is difficult to work for a long time in this industry without being a devout Christian.

That point may be quite obvious to someone pursuing a career as a Gospel artist, songwriter, or producer. When the primary content of your music is the message of the Gospel, and when so much of your life will be spent creating and performing that music, it is easy to understand why your convictions must be in line with your material.

That point may *not* be so obvious for someone pursuing a career as an industry professional. For us, why would a corporate job in Gospel music differ from a corporate job in any other industry in the world? The answer is found in this third sector.

When so much of the business of Gospel music must be conducted in connection with the Church Community, it becomes essential to understand, accept, and even embrace core ministry concepts in order to successfully interact within that world.

Several years ago, I had the wonderful opportunity to work with a nationally known and highly respected pastor. Our record company had entered into a business relationship with this gentleman that would enable him to create and produce albums featuring his church choir and showcasing several artists who had become involved with his ministry over the years.

The pastor was a brilliant innovator and accomplished businessman who had been wise enough to surround himself with a staff capable of maintaining and advancing the various divisions within his large organization. However, the Gospel music industry was a new frontier for them.

In my role as publicity and promotions director, I had the duties of planning and executing local and national media and radio campaigns for the projects under this new deal. The first order of business was to build a relationship with the pastor and his staff in preparation for introducing the new deal to my media and radio contacts.

After a few on-site visits and meetings with the pastor and his staff, I quickly began to see that while the record company deal was an important goal for them, the vast majority of their organization was focused on spiritual and social concerns, meeting the needs of hundreds of thousands of people in their city and around the world.

The ministry world was their primary forum. It impacted the decisions they made, the manner in which they set their priorities, and the language they spoke. They were used to viewing the world through their commitment and dedication to the work of the church. They were *not* accustomed to the unique considerations of the Gospel music industry.

In the early days, it was a bit challenging for me to get my new partners to understand why many of the tasks I had for them— selecting a publicity photo, approving the edit of a radio single, completing an interview with a local AM radio station—had any significance. Over time, as I began to outline the industry world for them, they grew to see those activities as another necessary step in furthering the vision of their pastor and broadening the reach of their ministry.

Ultimately, we worked well together and enjoyed great success with a series of projects. However, I am convinced it would not have been possible for us to create a system of cooperation and teamwork if I had not had a healthy regard for their ministry perspective. On many days, I would have become too frustrated to pursue my goals had I not had an equal devotion to both ministry and industry.

My commitment to my faith enabled me to understand their vision and helped me to learn their language. My respect for the Church Community motivated me to find ways to coordinate my business efforts with their ministry needs.

That example was quite specific, but I must say, I have found myself in similar situations throughout my career. Whether I was working with an artist who was also a pastor, planning a live recording at a church, or working to negotiate the terms of a ministry engagement for an artist, the overlap between the Business Community and the Church Community has required special skills and sensitivity to spiritual issues.

Over the years, I have found that those who would respect and embrace the lifestyle of Christianity have been able to maintain longevity in the Gospel Business Community. Those who have found that challenge either unnecessary or unappealing soon move on to other musical marketplaces.

I don't believe it is as simple as a spiritual shortcoming on the part of those who move on. In reality, the implications of the Church Community are often at odds with the needs and goals of the Business Community. Issues of ministry and lifestyle make it more difficult to function freely in a business as image-focused, commercially-driven, and competitive as the music industry.

In my own work, the primary motivator for pushing through to overcome those difficulties is my sense of calling, which is rooted in my personal relationship with God. Although it can be hard, I have made a commitment to sacrifice everything for that relationship, including, at times, my business goals.

Sometimes in the short term, the sacrifice of those goals means that I take an apparent loss. But I have seen that, in the long term, God rewards my commitment in ways beyond my imagination.

For me, that level of faith was born in my church experience. It is a ministry concept that became the backbone for my business life and has made it possible for me to make a long career of my work in Gospel music. For that, I am truly grateful.

As we close our discussion of the three sectors of the Gospel music industry, I want to stress how important I believe it is to understand and value each sector equally. Whether you are aspiring to be a member of the Creative Community or a member of the Business Community, I hope you will take the time to learn about and appreciate each community within the Gospel music industry. I truly believe our success as a marketplace depends upon our ability to reconcile the goals and needs of artistry, industry, and ministry.

Part Two:

For The Aspiring Artist

The Call To Artistry

Let me reiterate this fact: For every one aspiring industry executive I've ever met, I have easily met fifty aspiring artists. I believe that is true for a variety of reasons—visibility of the Creative Community overall, the dream of celebrity, and the attractiveness of the creative process, to name a few. Quite simply, when most people think of the music industry, they think of singers, songwriters, and producers.

It's no wonder someone trying to break into the industry would want to be among that group of people. Artists are the cool kids, the ones everyone wants to call his friend or hang out with. In the Gospel music industry, that is no different.

In fact, in many ways that draw may be a bit greater due to the high level of talent among Gospel artists and because of the attraction of "the anointing." We all love to feel the power of a really great Gospel song or experience the electricity of a truly powerful Gospel performance. Even outside of Gospel audiences, that is true.

Think about the number of times you've seen a Gospel or even Gospel-inspired performance on a mainstream TV show. No matter how mediocre that performance may seem to a Gospel music aficionado, it will almost always end in a standing ovation.

Often merely the appearance of choir robes on stage can guarantee there will not be a dry eye or a member of the audience still seated when the song ends!

I say that with some degree of humor, but the fact that we can all relate to that experience it is a testament to the power of the music. So of course it would be highly attractive to be on the giving end of that power. To take the stage and sing your heart out to a crowd who is visibly moved is a dream I completely understand.

Nevertheless, to merely dream that dream is not enough. The dream requires long-term commitment and years of work, not only honing your musical gifts, but developing a proficiency in public ministry and at least a working knowledge of the music business.

I do not say those things to overwhelm or discourage you. On the contrary! Knowing the truth about what will be involved early in your process will save you years of frustration, enable you to remain focused in failure, and equip you to handle your successes.

If you've spent some time in reflection and you truly believe the Creative Community of the Gospel music industry is your long-term goal, this section is for you.

Necessary Elements

On any Sunday, in almost every city in America, some of the most gifted singers the world has ever seen will take the stage in their local churches. They will move the audience, draw people to their feet, perhaps even change a few lives. They will bless your soul with the agility of a run, the strength of tone, thickness of voice, or ability to interpret the moment with their unique phrasing.

All of them are gifted singers. Most of them will never become successful[1] recording artists.

Becoming a successful artist *begins* with being a gifted singer or musician. However, to that gift you must add several key elements. Chief among those are:

- World-class Talent
- A Distinct Message
- A Unique Image
- Spiritual Maturity
- Business Savvy
- Patience
- Persistence

---

[1] For the purposes of this discussion, I am defining success as commercially viable with a national following, similar to the success of most well-known Gospel artists.

Although those key elements may appear to be self-explanatory, I believe they warrant a closer look.[2]

Necessary Element: World-class Talent

Throughout my career as I have traveled to churches across the country, and as I have received countless demo packages from aspiring artists, I have grown to see that there is a distinction between gifted singers and musicians and those with **world-class talent**. To be the best in your church or the best in your city are wonderful accomplishments. And for artists who have developed their gifts to that point, there are numerous opportunities to share their music and ministries within their local or regional marketplaces.

In fact, over the years I have met several examples of artists who are able to subsidize their income or even make their sole living from local and regional artistry. They perform at local churches and at concerts in their area, get airplay on their local Gospel radio stations, appear on local TV shows, and even release and sell independently produced CDs. It takes hard work to be organized enough to accomplish all of that. Their efforts are not to be taken lightly.

It is important to know whether you are called by God to be a local, regional or national artist. This is perhaps the most essential question for the aspiring artist, for one key reason: The appropriate grace will accompany your calling.

---

[2] **One quick programming note:** Throughout this section, I will often refer to an artist as "he." This is in no way to indicate that the majority of artists are men. It is simply easier to speak in the universal gender. If I were to interrupt you every few seconds with "he or she," or "his or her," you would soon wander off to other reading. It is my goal to keep you glued to this little book. So I hope you'll indulge me.

The artist with a local or regional calling who insists on pursuing national artistry will often be met with frustration. The artist with a national calling who attempts to function purely on the local and regional level will be met with equal frustration. I'm sure we can all think of examples of artists who were hometown heroes but never seemed to get that big break. But over the course of my career, I have also seen examples of artists with a national calling, who had very little effectiveness within the music ministries of their home churches. The grace they experienced before a crowd of thousands did not seem to translate as well before hundreds.

Strange though it may seem, this phenomenon makes perfect sense.

In my own life, I have found that I have the most success when I function within the realm of my calling. I am not afraid to try other things. But when I began to understand more about the plan of God for my life, I discovered He gave me success in direct proportion to my obedience to Him. The moment I committed to my calling at the expense of my personal desires, God began to open doors, reveal opportunities, and add blessing to my efforts in ways I had simply never experienced before.

With that in mind, I want to encourage you to embrace whoever you are called to be. There is no shame in not scoring a major record deal if your calling is to local or regional artistry. In fact, the great shame is to function outside of your purpose. Not only will you struggle in your efforts, you will not have the resources of heaven to help you.

How does this apply to the issue of world-class talent?

Quite simply, the goal of the Gospel music industry is to launch *national* artistry. The target audience for albums released by any major record company—and most independently owned record companies as well—is always going to be a *national* audience. Therefore, it stands to reason that those companies will always look for artists with world-class talent and potential to have the broadest impact.

It is unfortunate, but many times what is celebrated among the hometown crowd will not translate well to a national audience. To use a metaphor from the world of sports: Being the fastest runner at your high school does not ensure you will be the fastest runner at the Olympics. To measure oneself by a limited group of similar people is to set a dangerously low standard. Indeed there is a value to broad influence and the pressure of competition. It's the same with musical gifts.

Let me offer another example from my early life.

I have already mentioned that I grew up in a musical family. I also had the great fortune to be raised in a church where music was considered an essential part of the ministry. There were choirs of all ages and many variations of vocal groups. Our national organization even had its own marching band!

Through the years, I admired the older kids who began to excel at keyboards and songwriting and formed ensembles within our church. The songs they sang and the musical arrangements they created built upon the musical foundation I had already received from my parents. Those people were my heroes because they were my first exposure to Gospel music outside of my home.

When my sister became an adult, she moved on from our family's church and joined another church organization. To my surprise, they were even more musical than we were.

My sister's church had given rise to a few national recording artists, enabling several of their young musicians to get a taste of life as professional players. These were guys in their late teens and early 20s, but when they played, it sounded exactly like what I heard on albums by Andraé Crouch and The Winans.

It blew my mind that regular people could play that well. Slowly, my ideas about music began to change.

Those young guys were gifted, but what took their gifts to that next level was exposure to venues and other musicians beyond their hometown. The skills of musicians they met on the road and the standard of excellence demanded by the recording artists they accompanied forced them to mature in their gifts.

At home, it was easy to be the best in the room. On the road, everyone they met was the best in their respective rooms! To keep up with that new, higher standard, they were now challenged to become better musicians.

I've seen the same phenomenon at work countless times with singers. A singer may be the greatest talent within his home church. However, most of the time it is not until that singer begins to get exposure working with other singers and musicians beyond his borders that his talent really begins to develop. That kind of development is essential for those who aspire to become recording artists.

The standard on the national level is inherently higher than standards on the local and regional levels. Therefore, it will take a higher level of skill to stand out in the national realm.

How exactly can you determine if you have world-class talent? There is no easy answer to this question. However, the best way to begin testing the waters is to increase your circle of influence. Here are three quick ways to do just that:

Listen to and network with other aspiring singers, musicians, and songwriters outside of your church organization

and hometown. In the age of social networking sites such as Myspace and Facebook, reaching out in this way has never been easier. The opportunity to explore the music pages of other singers and musicians and to connect directly to those individuals is only a few mouse clicks away.

Attend and participate in local and regional talent competitions and open-mic nights. Don't simply aim to win a prize; pay close attention to your fellow artists. There are many lessons to be learned from them—positive and negative.

Go to workshops and conferences targeted toward aspiring artists. Be willing to invest the registration fees and travel costs, and consider purchasing whatever materials—books, tapes, DVDs—may be available for sale.

To get the most from opportunities like these, it is important to remember that your immediate goal is not simply to be heard. You will be heard, but at this point in your career, it is far more valuable for you to listen and exchange ideas with others. The broader your influences and the stiffer your competition, the more you will be challenged to grow and develop.

Most people are not born with world-class talent. Just like in the sports world, true champions aspire to greatness, honing their skills by training and playing on increasingly competitive fields.

Necessary Element: A Distinct Message

As we spend time working on the creative aspects of artistry, we can never forget that the ultimate goals of Gospel music are to spread the message of the Gospel of Jesus Christ, to be an expression of worship to God and to bring hope and encouragement to believers.

The *message* is the distinguishing mark of our genre of music. Our style of music may overlap with musical styles in the mainstream and our method of delivery may be similar, but the content of our songs should always set us apart from every other form of music. The message is why we are here.

Beyond the general message of the Gospel, however, I truly believe every artist should have a **distinct message** of their own, a unique point of view that informs their artistry on every level. From the choice of songs on the albums to the primary focus of in-person ministry opportunities, an artist should have a story.

Within months of landing your first record deal, you will soon learn the importance of that concept, as the marketing team at your record company begins to put together a campaign to launch your debut album. The choice of radio single and images may inform the advertisements, sales pages etc., but inevitably, the publicist will need to write a bio.[3] In that moment, you will likely consider for the first time whether you have an interesting story to tell.

The writing of the first bio is a wonderful rite of passage for new artists. To look into your past and take that first stab at explaining who you are in an in-depth interview with a stranger makes you think about things you've likely not thought of in quite that way before.

Even if you don't feel you've unfolded that story in a particularly engaging manner, a good bio writer should be able to spice it up a bit for you. Hopefully the writer won't lie, but if he is successful in framing your story, he will have helped you to think about yourself in an objective way, which will serve you well in other interviews and on countless stages across America.

---

[3] "Bio" is short for biography. It is an article written about the artist, including basic background information and details about the album project that is being introduced. It is normally included in a press kit sent to members of the media as a way of gaining publicity opportunities.

On those stages, regardless of the genre of music, it is the obligation of every artist to be able to engage an audience of strangers with his music and through "talk time" between songs. In Gospel music, that obligation is particularly important because our music will almost always be performed within the context of church ministry.

The same way that people go to church to hear a life-affecting message, they will come to your concerts expecting to be changed in some way. They may love your record and know your songs, but when they come to see you live—especially if they have *paid* to see you—they will want to get a sense of who you really are in a way that impacts them.

The primary manner in which you will accomplish that is not by killing them with a run. Unless you are performing before a crowd of other singers, that will only get you so far. The primary manner in which you will impact your audiences is by having a distinct message.

A few years ago, I had the wonderful, rare opportunity to stand witness as one of my artists developed her distinct message. This artist had already completed the launch of her solo career, with the release of a critically acclaimed, commercially successful debut album. That album resulted in two hit songs and multiple award nominations both in and outside of the core Gospel music arena. The artist also landed the opportunity to be the opening act for one of the most highly anticipated concert tours of that year. National TV appearances and headlining concerts continued as she began preparing to record her follow-up album.

Several months into recording that second album, my artist began struggling to sing. Normal recording sessions and rehearsals were followed by extended periods of hoarseness. She pressed on and worked as much as she could until one day, about four weeks from the deadline to deliver the album, my phone rang.

As the A&R person[4] for the project, I picked up the phone expecting a general financial question or an update on the progress of the recording schedule. Instead, it was the producer of the album calling me to let me know they could not continue. The artist's vocal struggles had progressed until she could no longer attempt to record.

The producer then handed the phone to my artist, and in a truly heartbreaking moment, I listened as one of the most vibrant and hopeful people I've ever known wrestled with despair.

She went to a doctor a few days later and was diagnosed with vocal nodules, a potentially career-ending condition for which a very risky surgery is the only known cure. The surgery can either be successful, or result in the irreparable loss of a singer's voice.

In an act of faith, the artist decided not to have the surgery. Her primary source of income gone, she entered a costly vocal rehab program and spent the next year fighting a physical, financial, spiritual, and psychological battle I will never fully know.

I'd like to tell you that after a year, she was fully restored and moved forward as if nothing had ever happened. In reality, when she returned to the studio a year later, she was bruised and shaken and had to believe God for every note she sang.

It may seem like a tragic twist to a promising career, but in the months I worked with this artist during her return to the studio, I witnessed faith and determination unlike anything I had ever seen before.

It took us about four months to complete what we hadn't been able to attempt in more than a year. And over the following months,

---

[4] For a complete description of A&R, go to page 132.

as I watched the artist begin to share her testimony—first in her bio, then in countless interviews, and finally on stages around the world—I finally understood the impact of having a distinct message.

On her debut album, my artist may have had special skill and a fresh sound. But after her tragedy, she had substance and depth that can only come from a next-level encounter with God. Her story of overcoming and healing added power to her performances. She also had a new compassion for people, which brought warmth to her ministry.

For this artist, having a distinct message made all the difference in the types of songs she wrote and the direction of her albums. That message also began to open very different doors in terms of the kind of ministry invitations she received and the types of people who began attending her shows. Her message helped her to find a distinctive place for her artistry within the industry and within the ministry world.

While this story serves as a good illustration, I don't mean to imply that every artist must experience great loss in order to have a successful career. Not everyone will have that kind of story to tell. Nevertheless, I do believe it is terribly important for you, as an aspiring artist, to contemplate what unique experiences shape or "inform" your gift.

Hundreds of new artists are introduced each year. One big step toward distinguishing your artistry and beginning to establish your particular ministry is developing a distinct message.

Necessary Element: A Unique Image

It has always been interesting to me that **image**—the element of artistry to which the *most* attention is given in mainstream music—is given so little attention by aspiring Gospel artists. And too often, what little attention *is* given to the concept of image is sadly misdirected.

Most of us have watched mainstream videos and seen CD covers and witnessed the bold manner in which popular artists reflect and set trends with their clothing, hair, and makeup. But how exactly can we apply this to Gospel artistry?

When I was a teenager, there was one moment that forever reshaped my concept of the value of image for Gospel artists. Oddly enough, it was the album cover of a group I had only heard one time on the radio, and even then had mistaken for another of my favorite groups.

Somehow I found this LP and purchased it right away. Sitting at home in front of the stereo, the thing that impacted me as much as this group's new sound, was a truly revolutionary photo on the album cover.

There before me were six fresh-faced young men who didn't look too much older than my big sister, each with trendy haircuts, dressed in acid washed denim and black leather. Who *were* these guys? They played *Gospel*?

Now, I have already shared how I spent countless hours during my childhood in front of that stereo reading liner notes and looking at album covers. I had marveled at images of Andraé Crouch barefoot on the beach in jeans and an apple cap, or The Winans in their matching white sweaters, up close, sitting at a grand piano, or even the legendary Danniebelle Hall with that amazing smile, curly afro, and green satin blouse, leaning over the piano where she wrote so many classic songs.

All of those images were indelible in my memory. But with their debut album, *I'm Going On,* Commissioned forever uncovered for me the value of image.

It wasn't just that they were *not* in suits, standing on a mountain and pointing toward heaven. With that album cover, for the first time I felt a true connection between the way a Gospel artist looked, the way they sounded, and the message in their songs.

It was if they were saying, "We're saved, but we're cool, and we have something real to say to you." They had something real to say to *me*—not my parents.

I have to tell you, at that moment I opened my ears to their music and their lyrics in a way I never had to any group before. And for the next decade, album after incredible album, I felt like I was part of an ongoing conversation with those guys.

Most contemporary Gospel music lovers would agree that Commissioned was phenomenal for their harmonies, their skill as a band, and their classic songwriting. But I would argue that what made them legendary was the way they connected with their audience. They knew who they were; they knew their target audience and they understood the importance of making that message clear in every aspect of their artistry—right down to their look.

Nearly twenty years after I bought that album, I had the opportunity to attend the Commissioned Reunion live recording, which became a CD and DVD. It was one of the best concerts I have ever attended—and I have attended A LOT of concerts!

The most amazing thing was that in a truly standing-room-only crowd of about 3500, every person there knew every word to every song for 2½ hours. The crowd's reactions were virtually in sync. From the first word of each song, it was as if we were all reliving the same memories. It was more than merely loving Commissioned's music. Over the years, our lives had been deeply impacted by the culture of Commissioned.

Obviously image isn't the only factor in this. The members of Commissioned were and remain some of the most talented Gospel songwriters, producers, and artists who have ever lived. But the connection to their national audience certainly took a big leap with that first album cover.

Based on the photo alone, my parents and their friends would never have purchased that album for themselves. In fact, years later when I actually had the chance to hear Fred Hammond, a founding member of Commissioned, talk about this, he mentioned that the denim and leather placed them in controversy with many older churchgoers at that time.

But Commissioned's commitment to being exactly who they were, and to accurately represent that in their choices of hairstyle and clothing helped them to quickly connect to an audience. For the consumer, Commissioned's image took a lot of the guesswork out of who they were and what they were about.

Perhaps it would be hard for an aspiring artist today to be as cutting edge as Commissioned was in the early '80s. Since we live in an age of envelope pushers, to shock or surprise today's consumer requires levels of risk that might not be representative of Christianity. Nevertheless, the need for an artist to be physically consistent with his sound and message has not changed.

As an aspiring artist, you must never forget that the burden to connect to an audience falls on *you* rather than on the audience. It may be difficult to hear, but the truth is the audience has no real incentive to come to you. There are too many voices and ministries already competing for their hard-earned money, time and attention.

However, if you have a timely message and a calling from the Lord to do this, then *you* have the incentive to reach that audience. You *must* connect to them for your music and ministry to find a home. Once you know who you are and what you have to say, you can take some of the work out of it for the audience by having a strong, consistent image.

Now for the big question (drum roll here): **HOW**?

The easy answer would be to find a quality styling team—clothing stylist, hair stylist, and make-up artist. Someday when you've really broken through, perhaps that will be within your budget. Or, if you are fortunate enough to have a marketing director at your record company who truly knows his game, you may have the opportunity to experience such a team on the photo shoots for your CDs.

But the best answer to this question is much simpler. It begins where so many early steps in your career will begin—by asking yourself some key questions. Among those questions are the following:

Who am I?

Who do I believe I am called to reach? (Who's my target audience?)

What are my *strongest* physical traits?

What are my *weakest* physical traits?

What hair and clothing truly look good on me?

What hair and clothing do *not* look good on me?

What am I *comfortable* wearing?

A few of those will be easier for you to answer than others. All of them are basic questions that have very little apparent connection to music or ministry. They are important, however, because they require you to consider not only your overall appearance, but the manner in which others will perceive you.

An example: When you know that you are called to reach young women through your music and ministry, your appearance will need to be consistent with what young women find appealing. Your image will need to be something to which that audience relates in order to make them feel as if you have something relevant to say to them.

I'm not suggesting you raid the Juniors section of Marshall's or pattern your image after the hottest secular artist with a female teen fan base. First of all, those choices might not work well with your body shape. Secondly, those choices may be inappropriate for the venues where you will minister.

What I *am* suggesting is this: Knowing that young women are your target audience probably means you shouldn't be dressed too formally, with long, churchy dresses and your hair in a French roll all the time. Those looks are amazing on some of my favorite, more mature Gospel artists, but they might not be appropriate for you.

Since most of us have a hard time seeing ourselves objectively, it is helpful to keep a few close friends around you who have a good eye for style and a sincere heart toward you. It is invaluable if they are also good at being *gently* honest with you. (You should maintain friendships like that at all costs!)

Ultimately your look is something that will evolve throughout your career. You will change—and hopefully grow—as both a person and an artist, and so will your audience. The thing that won't change is the need to *consider* your look. As long as this portion of your life is lived in the public eye, it would service you well to embrace the notion of image.

Necessary Element: Spiritual Maturity

One of the most overlooked requirements for Gospel artists is the need for spiritual maturity. I believe the reason for this is simple:

Aspiring artists rarely consider that the call to Gospel music is—more often than not—a call to full-time ministry.

Now before you throw this little book across the room, please allow me to explain.

In our earlier discussion of the Church Community, we established that the main manner in which Gospel artists share their music and support sales of their CDs is by live performances. It stands to reason, therefore, that any aspiring Gospel artist should expect to spend a great deal of time in live performances before church congregations.

To develop the necessary skills to effectively reach people within those venues, an artist must become proficient in public ministry. Likewise, true proficiency in ministry requires **spiritual maturity**.

During the early days of your career—even after you have been blessed to release your first CD—it is likely you will *not* have opportunities to perform on the largest stages with special lighting and high quality sound systems. More than likely you will *not* have a choreographer or dancers around you either. Most of the time, you will stand on a simple church stage, with a standard sound system, room lighting, and perhaps your own performance tracks as accompaniment.

Under those circumstances, your talent may keep an audience's attention for a while. But what will bless the lives of the people and make them want to bring you back is how well you communicate the Gospel. Sharing your testimony in a meaningful way, the manner in which you introduce and explain your songs, and your ability to get an audience involved in your performance will make the lasting impression.

Looking at the picture I've just painted, it may be easy to conclude that *showmanship* is the skill at work here. After all, if you've ever been to a well-known mainstream recording artist's performance, you've seen many of those same skills at work. I would offer the following: In the mainstream, the audience has come to the event purely as entertainment. Within the church world, however, often the audience has come to the event with spiritual needs. Even if the church crowd hopes to be entertained, there is an inherent expectation for something deeper. Consequently, the burden on the Gospel artist is far different than that of his mainstream counterpart.

In the same way that a congregation comes to church every week expecting the pastor to have a fresh word from the Lord, your audiences will come to your concerts looking for something fresh and powerful. It may seem unfair, but they will expect you to sound just like your album and to bring a level of ministry that enhances what they've heard on your CDs.

Within your own power, that will rarely be possible. But when you live as if your artistry is your calling, your efforts and time will be spent on developing the necessary level of spiritual maturity to meet that calling. When you choose to live beyond your talent and truly embrace your calling, you will learn that effectiveness in public ministry requires a lifestyle of dedication and growth that comes from spiritual maturity.

Unfortunately, there are no shortcuts to spiritual maturity. You can certainly be taught to communicate well in front of people. And it is a given that as an aspiring artist you should be constantly honing your musical skills. But what about developing sensitivity for the flow of a service, having the compassion to listen to the tearful testimony of a fan, or simply the ability to be open and genuine in front of a room full of strangers? Showmanship will help you, but the heart of those skills will be born and developed as a result of your personal work away from public eyes. I'm not talking about closed rehearsals. I'm talking about the time spent one-on-one with God, building a personal relationship with Him and working on your own issues. That is the place where you will grow and mature and become equipped in ways no one can teach you.

To enhance your private walk, I would encourage anyone aspiring to national artistry to become a member of and active in a local church. Your pastor and your fellow church members should be a source of encouragement and prayer, and they should provide a spiritual covering for you as you move forward in your career.

It could become easy to see these particular requirements as unnecessary burdens. Rest assured, the commitment you make in this area will enable you to maximize your success. Spiritual maturity will give you the balance and character necessary to handle the pressures of national artistry.

I know celebrity, money, and influence are things we all *think* we want, but to handle those things without being destroyed and without compromising your standards requires spiritual maturity. Having that foundation is the only safeguard against losing the great blessings God has for you.

One important note: It may be true that some segments of the Gospel music industry are centered on the concept of Christian entertainment, rather than ministry. I would be among the first to admit there is a need for wholesome music and clean messages in current-day America.

Nevertheless, as world crises are more personally threatening and times have become immeasurably harder, people are beginning to search more urgently for answers. These days when audiences turn to Christian messages—whether through church services, music, movies, or books—they no longer want merely to be entertained. They want to hear words of comfort, hope, and truth from the people who are supposed to know about those things.

It would be a shame for them to turn to us and discover that we have nothing to say.

The only safeguard against that is to invest in your own spiritual growth. Take the time to become a person of substance. Accept the challenge to become spiritually mature.

Necessary Element: Business Savvy

Earlier I mentioned that members of the Creative Community are often uncomfortable with the industry side of music. Many elements of the music business are unnecessarily complicated and can be intimidating whether you're just getting started or a veteran of the professional music world. In the digital age, things have become more complicated than ever.

So I understand the glazed look in the eyes of my artists when I mention recording contracts or publishing agreements, producer points, or sync licenses. I truly sympathize with their urge to run at the mere mention of the words "work for hire."

The music industry is far from user friendly. But ignoring it won't make it go away. Ignoring the business will only increase the likelihood that you will wake up one day without the benefits you expected to have after decades of hard work. Unfortunately, relying solely upon someone else to understand the business for you only increases the likelihood that a person you once genuinely trusted will become the focal point of your blame.

There's a way to avoid all that: Embrace the vision of yourself as a savvy business person. Instead of seeing yourself solely in the dimension of a creative talent, begin to see yourself as someone capable of learning and conducting good business.

A strong relationship with the Lord makes this part of the journey much easier. On my own I know very little, but with the Holy Spirit at my side, I have access to the great mysteries of the universe. God understands everything I do not. Since He has called me to this, He has a vested interest in my success.

But how to begin?

My favorite book to recommend to people who are serious about pursuing a career in the music industry is Donald S. Passman's *All You Need To Know About The Music Business*. It is, in my opinion, the most easy-to-read, comprehensive overview of the music industry ever created for the aspiring artist. I have purchased several editions for my own library, and I have gifted a few more copies to young music industry friends and people who were just beginning. Everyone I've ever met who has read the book has been helped by it immeasurably.

To my disappointment, however, I have had to accept that many aspiring artists and musicians will not commit to the 475 pages of that book. And since it does not specifically address Gospel music concerns, a few have trouble finding the information relevant to their specific situation. I believe that is a serious oversight.

We have discussed the special concerns and needs of the Gospel music marketplace. Nevertheless, the Gospel music industry is *still* the *music* industry. From a business standpoint, 90% of the issues and structures, procedures, and standards that affect the music industry are the same for us all, regardless of musical genre. Our differences tend to lie in the areas of creativity, marketing, and promotion. What we create, who makes up our audience, and the manner in which we sell those creations to that audience may be unique to Gospel music, but the business around our music functions in nearly the same way as business in the mainstream music industry. In fact, most Gospel record labels are divisions within mainstream record companies.

With those things in mind, learning to be wise in Gospel music business begins with learning about overall music business. The goal is not to master every detail of music business. For the aspiring artist, it is more important have a working knowledge of the business areas and issues that will affect your artistry and ministry. This important step should be part of your commitment to being a good steward over what God has given to you.

Eventually you will need to have a team of quality business people around you to take your career to higher levels, but I would recommend you become and remain informed enough about business to properly choose that team and to accurately evaluate the advice you receive from them.

Below are three key recommendations for any aspiring artist seeking to increase his music business knowledge.

Recommendation: Read CD Packaging.

The easiest, most cost-effective way to begin learning about the music business world is to read the label copy (production notes, publishing, and record company credits) of your CDs. Feel free to laugh if you must, but there is no faster way to become familiar with key people, key companies, key roles, and the relationships between the parts than by reading the CD booklets and outside notes that come with your CD.

I know that in an iTunes world we believe CD booklets are a thing of the past, but as long as you can still buy physical CDs in stores and on-line, you should. Leave the downloading to your friends. If you are serious about breaking into this industry, you need to know as much as you can about the music that is out there and the people who are already doing what you are trying to do.

In the simple bits of information provided in CD booklets, you will find:

- Key record company personnel (along with addresses and web sites)
- Producer names and production companies
- Songwriter names and songwriter's associations (BMI, ASCAP, SESAC)
- Publishing companies
- Manager names and management companies (often with phone numbers, addresses, and web sites)
- Contact information for booking agencies
- The artist's team members and influences (see "**Thank Yous**")
- Lyrics of songs (**key study material for aspiring songwriters!!**)

With all of that information included at no additional cost, purchasing a physical CD is one of the smartest investments any aspiring artist could make. Furthermore, from a spiritual standpoint, there is no better way to ensure God will bless your music than by taking the time to buy someone else's CD. There is real-world value to the principle of sowing and reaping.[5]

Recommendation: Buy An Industry Source Book.

One of the most valuable resources for any aspiring artist is an industry source book. These types of publications are listings of key information, including contact information for record labels, management companies, booking agencies, radio stations, TV shows, retail outlets and churches, along with top artists, producers, and songwriters. The publications also include dates and information for key industry events (conferences, award shows, etc.).

The two most significant examples of this style of publication are the following:

1. The Gospel Music Industry Round-Up

(Published by Eye On Gospel Publications, *www.gospelroundup.com*)

2. GMA's Christian/Gospel Industry Directory

(Published by The Gospel Music Association, *www.gospelmusic.org*)

Both publications are available for order by mail or on-line for under $25. They are updated and published annually.

Contact information for various industry outlets might be appealing to you in terms of who to call looking for that first break. However, it's probably not appropriate to "cold call" a name from those source books or to start sending your music out to the companies listed there right away. First impressions are terribly important and this industry tends to be very small.

---

[5] Give, and it will be given to you. A good measure, pressed down, shaken together and running over, will be poured into your lap. For with the measure you use, it will be measured to you. (Luke 6:38, *NIV*)

So, use wisdom and wait for opportunities to build relationships. (More about that later.)

Rather than providing email addresses for your eblasts, industry source books can help you to gain a better sense of the parts of the industry and the manner in which those parts fit together in the real world. You will soon learn that having an accurate concept will not only aid you in making the right steps at the proper time, it will help you to make the most of each step as you take it.

Always remember your accurate concept of the industry—or lack thereof—has a way of shining through. Valuable opportunities and connections to key people may be gained or lost as a result of the first impression you make. Prepare yourself for those pivotal moments by doing your homework.

Recommendation: Do An Internship At A Record Label.

The best crash course in real-world music industry business is an internship at an established record label. Before you read any further, let me clarify something: An aspiring artist should NOT do an internship at a record company for the chance to get his demo into the right hands.

In my experience, nothing is more of a turn-off to music industry executives than the intern who comes in the door looking for his big break. And in all my years at record companies, I have yet to see a person get their big break from being an intern.

So why am I suggesting you do an internship?

Quite simply, there is no better way to learn how artists are signed, albums are made, album projects are completed, and those finished projects are promoted and marketed. And, unfortunately, you will probably not have the opportunity to see that process in action once you actually have a record deal.

Signed artists rarely get to see the daily activities at their record companies.

A signed artist is handled gingerly, given hard facts with a careful hand, with key information communicated to him through his team members (management, etc.). Even in instances where an artist has more hands-on interaction with his record company, viewing the process from the perspective of a signed artist makes it difficult to evaluate that process *objectively*.

Don't get me wrong. I understand the challenging experience of spending months, sometimes years creating a very personal work of art and having to release that work to a system that will evaluate and assess it dispassionately, based primarily upon its commercial value. It is painful to have something so close to your heart treated that way. Objectivity is not the operative posture at that moment.

However, I also understand the challenge of having to represent, promote, and sell a creative work in an increasingly hostile commercial environment. It is extremely hard to sell a large quantity of CDs in today's marketplace, and equally as hard to explain to artists why sales of their project may not be going according to plan.

My point is this: The Creative and Business Communities are two sides of the same music industry coin. Each side has unique challenges. Ironically, the very qualities that make artists and industry people great within their respective areas are often the same qualities that keep them from truly understanding each other's needs and goals. That lack of understanding can lead to a great deal of tension, particularly when times are hard.

Completing an internship with a record company *before* your own album is at stake will grant you the luxury of objectivity, thereby helping you understand the roles, goals, and needs of record companies and their employees.

It may not seem important to you now, but when you finally have your record deal, these people will be a necessary alliance for you. There is no better way to prepare for successfully negotiating your way through that relationship than taking the time to learn about their roles within the context of their world.

Furthermore, the more you know about the industry process before you complete your first album, the easier it will be to deal with the pressures of that process when *your* art and ministry are on the line.

One final note: Unpaid internships are equally as valuable as paid internships. Sure, it would be great to have a significant experience and also get a check for your effort, but where that is not an option, I would still encourage you to embrace the opportunity. Your willingness to invest in yourself will yield far more than financial dividends.

Necessary Element: Patience

If you're anything like me, just the heading of this little subsection made you a bit testy. One of my least favorite things in the whole world is when someone tells me to be patient. I don't like being patient, and I rarely see the need for patience when I am already focused, passionate, and believe I am ready for whatever challenge presents itself. Consequently, one of the areas where God has had to work on me the most—and longest—is in proving to me the value of patience.

Some years ago, I saw a scripture in the book of Romans that has turned out to be one of the greatest assets to my walk in Christ:

...we glory in tribulations also: knowing that tribulation worketh patience; and patience, experience; and experience, hope: And hope maketh not ashamed; because the love of God is shed abroad in our hearts by the Holy Ghost which is given unto us. (Romans 5:3–5, KJV)

The first time I noticed this scripture was in church during a sermon. I have to confess, I don't remember exactly what the sermon was about, but I do remember realizing, as I read those words that God had a **growth plan** for me. It was His divine goal that my tests and trials should produce patience, which would produce experience (or "character" according to the *NIV*) and in turn, that would create hope in me.

This growth dynamic has played out in my personal life. However, I have been able to identify the dynamic at work most clearly in my professional life. The tests and challenges I have endured in my career and ministry have truly allowed me to see the value of patience.

As a life-long student of the Gospel music industry, I have also had the phenomenal opportunity to watch this dynamic at work in the careers and ministries of many artists. This is especially true in the first area of growth outlined in Romans 5:3—the transition from tribulation to patience.

Most of us are familiar with the term "overnight success." Nearly as many of us have seen interviews with artists, who have *apparently* come to national prominence quickly, explain why they were *not* in fact overnight successes. They've shared with Jay or Conan or Dave how they had been performing for many years, playing wherever they could before that big break finally came.

What is true for mainstream music is *especially* true for Gospel music. There simply are no overnight successes.

Look at any major Gospel artist today, and the success you are seeing is the product of more than ten years of hard work and experience. And for those artists at the very top of the field, you're likely looking at a history of more than twenty years. Their biggest hit may have catapulted them to prominence, but believe me, they've been at this thing for a while.

I began this section by focusing on the verse in Romans because it is so easy to look at the processes we go through and become frustrated when we do not yet see the success of which we've dreamed. However, when you recognize that the entire process is designed by God, each step depositing in us a different quality necessary for the next level, you will come to view the road quite differently.

There are by-products of character and hope that will never fully form in us unless we submit patiently to our tests. And because this is ministry on a national level, you will find that in your season—at your moment of breakthrough—character and hope will be more necessary than you imagined.

Most of us have heard stories from the mainstream entertainment world of artists who were overcome by the weight of celebrity. There are numerous instances of creative geniuses self-destructing with alcohol or drugs or illicit relationships as a result of the pressures of fame. The stories may not be as widely known within the Gospel world, but the pressures of fame and national ministry can have the same effects.

What will make the difference in how we respond to success is our degree of character. Even though the process may be hard to understand, character is formed in us through the things we suffer and endure with patience. Our difficult times will give us the tools we need to survive our successes.

I love that the Apostle Paul ends this passage in Romans with a reference to God's love. So often the things we endure feel like punishment. It is never fun to be shaped and formed. But our God is a loving Father, intent on making sure we have everything we need both externally and internally.

So, be patient, my friend. The gifts inside of you will not spoil or expire. Take advantage of the process and get everything you can out of the time you are required to wait. In the end your success will be sweeter, both because of the way in which your ministry will bless others and for the way in which the process has blessed you.

Necessary Element: Persistence

This final necessary element is, like patience before it, an issue connected to our character. While it is the last item on our list, in many ways I believe it is a core element, tying all the others together. Ultimately your success in any of the areas we've discussed—like the success of your overall ministry—will be the result of your continuous determination, your **persistence**.

It is important to draw a distinction between persistence and aggression. Too often over the course of my career, I have met individuals who believed the best way to gain success was by beating down every door and making demands of every person of influence until someone gave them a chance.

While determination is a key element to any breakthrough, I find those who focus primarily on aggressive techniques to create their opportunities only succeed at turning off anyone who would otherwise be willing to help. Even worse, I have watched as those same individuals, begrudgingly granted their opportunity, proved their talent and skill to be less than notable.

The time they spent calling and emailing, showing up at people's offices, and promoting themselves inappropriately, was time they were *not* spending actually becoming good enough, or prepared enough, to warrant the hype.

That's aggression. Persistence, on the other hand, is related to the manner in which you continue faithfully to develop and maintain the gifts, talents, skills, and knowledge necessary to accomplish your calling. The primary focus is on your creative efforts and your internal work, rather than on manufacturing opportunities to showcase your talent.

King Solomon in the book of Proverbs says, "A man's gift maketh room for him, and bringeth him before great men" (Proverbs 18:16 KJV). This means that when we place the emphasis on being the best steward we can be over the gifts God has given us, phenomenal opportunities will find us. We don't have to beat down the doors on our own behalf. God has ordained for opportunities to find *us*.

A friend in the Creative Community shares, as part of her testimony, the fact that she never created a demo, or shopped her talent to record companies. Instead, she served faithfully wherever she found herself—Sunday school, youth ministry, church choir, worship team—developing her gift and maturing in ministry. When she was ready to move forward in her career, offers and opportunities began to come to her. The breakthrough came and because she was persistent in her development, she was ready to make the most of it.

I am not suggesting you should avoid making a demo. In fact a few pages from now, you'll see why I think demo creation is an important step for the aspiring artist. What I *am* saying is this: Learn to value the process over the end result.

Accomplishing your goals is wonderful, but the longer you live, the more you will recognize that often the qualities required to be successful are developed within us through the long journey toward that success.

We're all familiar with this example in nature: A mother hen will lay her eggs and incubate them by sitting on her nest for an extended period. Nevertheless, she will leave the baby chicks to accomplish the challenging task of cracking through their shells on their own. Despite how difficult their struggle may appear, if they receive assistance, they will not develop the strength they need to survive outside of the shell. The act of persistence in breaking through their shells equips the chicks for survival.

It is the same with us. It's all about persistence. We persist because we have confidence that God will bring to pass the things He has spoken over our lives. When we are secure in that knowledge, it is easier to recognize that we don't have to take control of our timelines, wrestling opportunities to the ground. When we have mastered the balance of continuous determination, we are comfortable with the surety of God's grace over our lives and at work in our ministries.

The writer of Hebrews makes an exhortation particularly appropriate to this discussion. I'll let him have the last words here:

> So do not throw away your confidence; it will be richly rewarded. You need to persevere so that when you have done the will of God, you will receive what he has promised. (Hebrews 10:35–36 NIV)

First Steps

The Gospel music industry is not an exact science. There are no easy formulas for success or quick paths to stardom. Nevertheless, there are proven methods to increase your skill level and to be better prepared to find and take advantage of opportunities to launch your artistry on a national level.

Now that you have a more accurate overview of the Gospel music industry and the necessary elements for national artistry, it's time to take a look at some important first steps.[6]

Seek Out Ministry Opportunities.

This step is one of the easiest to accomplish, but also one of the least likely to be thought of in connection with launching your national artistry. For clarity, I'm not talking about looking for opportunities to share your talent. We will talk about that step in a minute.

For now, I'm suggesting you look for places to serve in *any* capacity in which you are needed. Depending on the world around you, this may not have anything to do with sharing your musical

---

[6] *Quick programming note:* I have chosen *not* to number these because there is no step-by-step plan for becoming a successful artist. Nevertheless, I have listed these particular steps in an order of priority that I believe will service you best.

talents. If your church is looking for volunteers to help with answering phones, assisting with children's ministry, helping seniors, or even cleaning bathrooms, you should consider extending your services. If your school or community is advertising for tutors or mentors or looking for volunteers to assist with food and clothing drives, you should be eager to sign up.

I recognize this may be a difficult concept to embrace. How in the world could a commitment to volunteerism increase your potential for success as a Gospel artist? The answer is simple: Real ministry begins hands-on and in direct response to the needs of people.

You must never forget that if you are called to be a Gospel artist, there will always be a *ministry* component to your work. Gospel artists must be excellent musically, but they should also have substance and skill in ministry. That ministry component is *not* optional if you expect to have a significant impact on people and longevity in the marketplace.

Talented singers will come and go; their success dependent upon the ebb and flow of the marketplace. However, an artist with an effective ministry can have a career lasting thirty years or more, with the ability to find success beyond CD sales and touring opportunities. With that in mind, your decision to develop the ministry side of your vision is one of the surest investments you can make.

Unfortunately, you cannot cram to learn effective ministry quickly *after* you've signed your first recording contract. The foundation for effective ministry starts long before that day, with service in your everyday world. Through simple acts of giving, you will develop both **compassion for people** and **the posture of a servant.**

Develop Compassion For People.

In our previous discussion of the importance of having a distinct message, I mentioned three primary goals for Gospel music. To recap, they were:

- To spread the message of the Gospel of Jesus Christ
- To be an expression of worship to God
- To bring hope and encouragement to believers

While the first two goals may be accomplished primarily through the content of your songs, the third goal is more interactive, with implications for the Gospel artist far beyond the music.

Your audience may draw hope and encouragement from the lyrics you sing or your delivery of your material, but the need to be inspired rarely ends when the CD stops playing or the curtain falls on one of your shows. Gospel music audiences expect to be encouraged and inspired by **you**.

Fans of Beyoncé may have all of her albums, posters, photos, and wear her line of clothes. They may visit her web site, go to her shows, or even try to sneak back stage for a chance to meet her. However, with secular fans, there is an expectation that the celebrity they so admire is untouchable. In fact, part of the draw is the expectation that their favorite artist is indeed a star, distant, shining, out of reach.

I think that is one of the reasons why in the instances where fans actually get to come into close proximity with their favorite stars, there are tears and screams and even fainting spells. (If you've ever watched Michael Jackson's European concert videos, or seen the reaction of the fans who visit Elvis Presley's Graceland on the anniversary of his death, you know what I mean.)

In Gospel music, I have seen another kind of behavior at work among the fans. Rather than a sense of separation from celebrity, Gospel music enthusiasts tend to display an overwhelming connectedness to their artists. It's as if the Gospel artist is an old friend whom they've known all of their lives, a distant relative with whom they've maintained a regular correspondence.

Often Gospel music fans are quite personal. They refer to their artists by first name. And when they approach for a photo or autograph, they step boldly, offering a story of the last time they met that artist or the ways in which they are closely linked to the artist. They offer heartfelt testimonies and long commentaries about the music and the artist's impact on their lives.

I have certainly witnessed more than a few instances of Gospel music fans taking this behavior to uncomfortable levels. In general, however, I am grateful that ours is a marketplace where our oneness as members of the Body of Christ takes precedence over the velvet rope of celebrity.

Although it may seem that I have completely digressed from the topic of compassion, I assure you I have not.

It is important for you as an aspiring artist to be aware of this environment. There is a built-in expectation that you will be accessible, willing to interact with the people who have welcomed you into their lives, and supported your art and ministry. And there is the additional weight that your interaction with your supporters should result in something spiritually significant for them as well.

It is not easy to pour out from the stage for thirty minutes or an hour and, afterward, have people anxious to touch you and have personal time with you when you are tired and sweaty. The expectations of fans can begin to feel like a burden after so many days on the road, away from your family and friends. I truly believe the only way to overcome that feeling is by developing a compassion for people.

It is interesting to me that in all of the records of Jesus' ministry, there is never an instance where He became weary of the masses. The Gospels provide evidence of His frustration with the religious leaders of His day, but throughout His ministry, He displayed a continuous ability to respond to the needs of everyday people.

And Jesus went about all the cities and villages, teaching in their synagogues, and preaching the gospel of the kingdom, and healing every sickness and every disease among the people. But when he saw the multitudes, he was moved with compassion on them, because they fainted, and were scattered abroad, as sheep having no shepherd. (St. Matthew 9:35–36, KJV)

Even after hours teaching and healing the sick, Jesus could look upon hundreds of people and continue to be touched by their needs. In fact, miracle after miracle, the Gospels record that Jesus' compassion was the catalyst for His powerful acts.[7]

We can never overlook the fact that Jesus used His alone time wisely. The Gospels outline instances of Jesus going away by Himself to pray.[8] It is likely that He was built up and refreshed for His work among the people during those times.

We should learn from Christ's example. It is important for us to pattern ourselves after Jesus and to allow the Holy Spirit to

---

[7] For other examples of this, please reference the following: St. Matthew 14:14, St. Matthew 18:27, St. Mark 1:41, St. Mark 6:34.

[8] See St. Matthew 14:23, St. Mark 6:46, St. Luke 6:12.

develop the character of our Lord in us. His image reflected in our lives is really the only worthwhile gift any of us has to offer.

Again, it is highly unlikely that you will be able to develop a sincere compassion for the masses *after* your first CD hits the stores. It is a difficult skill to acquire on the job, and unfortunately people tend to notice when they finally meet you in person—someone they have celebrated from afar and to whom they have developed a deeply personal connection—and you do not appear to value their support *from your heart*. That one impression is likely to be the only thing they remember about you.

It is far more beneficial for you to make a commitment to develop compassion as an authentic part of your character *before* you are in the public eye. A key part of this is accomplished by time spent alone in prayer, allowing the Holy Spirit to shape and develop your character. In addition you should look for opportunities to serve real people in the real world. It doesn't have to be anything broad-based or public. Begin by looking for little ways to be a blessing and be open to bigger doors that God will open, even if they require more of your time.

The time you spend learning to serve will never be wasted. Remember these people will someday be your audience. If you do not develop a genuine heart for their needs now, it is likely you will have difficulty connecting with them from the stage.

Develop The Posture Of A Servant.

Because the Gospel music marketplace is imbedded within the mainstream music industry, it can at times be difficult for us to see the important distinctions between the role of Gospel artists and that of their mainstream counterparts. The platform of national artistry may bring you some degree of fame and wealth, but those things should never be the primary motivation. In fact, if we were making a list in order of importance, even the chance to share your musical gift should fall behind the opportunity to touch people. Rather than to aspire to be a star, we should long for the posture of a servant.

Now I know that over the years servanthood has gotten a bad rap. You say the word servant to most people and immediately it conjures up images of slavery, abuse and being taken advantage of. It's a sensitive area and one in which the devil would love to keep us bound by our lack of understanding.

In truth, the role of a servant is highly celebrated in the Kingdom of God. And in our ministries we will find that God honors and exalts us in direct proportion to our submission to His will and our willingness to walk humbly among people.[9]

I know it is extremely tempting to believe concepts like that only apply to life within the church world, but I promise you the laws of God are relevant to our everyday lives and careers.

If you are struggling to believe me right now, let's take a look at some of the words of Jesus:

> "But he that is greatest among you shall be your servant. And whosoever shall exalt himself shall be abased; and he that shall humble himself shall be exalted. (Matt 23:11–12, KJV)

Jesus takes the time to teach that concept as a core principle to His closest disciples. They were not yet pastors or apostles. They were just everyday people from everyday backgrounds—doctors, fishermen, tax collectors, carpenters. He wasn't teaching them

---

[9] By humility and the fear of the Lord are riches, honor and life. (Proverbs 22:4, KJV)

principles for administering churches because there was no church at that time. He was giving real world principles to real world people just like you and me.

Jesus makes a point to demonstrate the principle of humility in a pivotal moment shortly before His crucifixion:

> *So after he had washed their feet, and had taken his garments, and was set down again, he said unto them, Know ye what I have done to you? Ye call me Master and Lord: and ye say well; for so I am. If I then, your Lord and Master, have washed your feet; ye also ought to wash one another's feet.*
>
> *For I have given you an example, that ye should do as I have done to you. Verily, verily, I say unto you, The servant is not greater than his lord; neither he that is sent greater than he that sent him.*
>
> *If ye know these things, happy are ye if ye do them. (John 13:12–17 KJV)*

We cannot see the washing of the disciples' feet as a simple act of ceremony. Jesus was not merely a peer whom the disciples respected, doing them a favor. By the time He tied a towel around His waist, bent down and began to wash their nasty, dusty toes they had already seen the Holy Spirit descend upon Him like a dove. They had watched Him walk on water and cast out demons, heal the worst diseases of their day and teach the deep things of scripture with power.

By that moment, they had come to revere Jesus as the most powerful person they had ever encountered. To them, He was a star, the most significant celebrity they had ever heard of. So the fact that He would extend His love to them in that way, so unexpectedly and without fanfare, demonstrated something about servanthood that would change their lives.

It should also change our perspective.

Your career as a Gospel artist may come with certain trappings of celebrity—performances on national stages, appearances on TV shows, your own videos, your photo in magazines. Those things may cause the public to view you as a star. But you must never forget the purpose for which God has called you. Your success, if it is to have true value, will never be about you. It will always be about Him being glorified through you.

Imagine the power of the moment, when a long-time fan meets you for the first time and instead of separating yourself with a stuffy attitude or a puffed up self-importance, you take the time to show love, to display humility. It may only be with a smile or the patience to take a photo, hear their testimony, or pray with them, but in that moment, you may have touched a life in a way you will never fully know.

I understand that it may be difficult to separate yourself from the fantasies you've held about artistry. And after years of patience and persistence, it is virtually impossible not to anticipate the day when you will achieve notoriety. There will be joy in that achievement. Nevertheless, I would encourage you to refocus your dream. The temporary thrill of those moments of fame will pale in comparison to the fulfillment you will have when you are sure the people in the audience have applauded, not simply because your talent is so wonderful, but because their lives have been changed.

Our greatest role will never be the role of celebrity. Our greatest role will be the role of a servant. It is a blessing to be called by God to serve people with your gift. The power to have a positive impact on countless lives through both your music and your ministry should never be taken lightly.

Do yourself a favor: Begin adjusting your posture now from that of future star to that of servant. In your prayer time, begin asking the Lord to reveal the character of Jesus in you. God will honor your humility by exalting you in your season.

Take Advantage Of Outlets For Performance.

One of the reasons Gospel artists are some of the best singers in the world is because our marketplace requires us to be amazing live *and* amazing in the studio. Gospel artists make CDs, but from the beginning of their lives—singing from an early age in their home churches—throughout the course of their careers, they also perform regularly in live settings.

Consequently, Gospel artists tend to excel at live performance. Truth be told, that is one of the reasons live albums remain a staple of the Gospel music industry, while they maintain a rare, "event" status in the mainstream marketplace.

To be equipped to deliver in-concert at a consistent level of quality, Gospel artists must "train" harder at the craft of live performance. Although regular rehearsals may prepare you to deliver your music well, they are limited in their ability to prepare you for many aspects of public performance, including talk time, interaction with an audience, ministry elements, and learning to remain within your allotted time.

Live performance will require you to become skilled in all of those areas. Therefore, it is essential for aspiring artists to seek out and take advantage of opportunities to perform in front of live audiences.

Clearly, church services and church events are the most accessible outlets for live performance. But don't limit yourself. Look for musicals, open-mic nights, and new artist showcases. It is *not* important for such opportunities to be paid engagements. Money is nice, but your greater need at this point in your career is stage time in front of people.

It is amazing how your skill set will grow simply by stepping out and using your gift. Pay attention to what connects with the audience and, even more importantly, what elements of your performance seem to fall flat. Listen, watch, and refine. And wherever possible, take that honest and gentle set of friends with you. It is so helpful to have someone you trust tell you how it looked and sounded from the audience.

It is highly beneficial to be able to work out the kinks in your presentation when so little is at stake for you. Eventually, you will be booked by promoters or churches and paid to give a high-quality performance. At that point, when real money and contracts, product sales, and future performance opportunities will be at stake, it will be too late to *begin* to develop your live skills.

Always remember: While you are believing God for your big break, you need to be actively preparing for it. Show your faith through your works. Don't wait for the day when your face will grace the cover of a CD. Get out there and begin to touch audiences right where you are, right now.

AND NOW FOR EVERYONE'S FAVORITE STEP... DRUM ROLL PLEASE!

Create A Demo.

I really try to avoid assuming, so for those of you who don't yet know what a demo is....

A "demo" is a demonstrational recording. It is a short collection of songs created by an aspiring artist, songwriter, or producer as evidence of their potential. Normally this material is sent to record companies, managers, or even promoters as a pitch for consideration. It is a tool created in an effort to have someone of influence learn about your talent and hopefully agree to work with you.

The summer before I was hired for my first job in the industry, I attended a national music conference sponsored by one of the largest Christian music organizations in the country. At the conference, I had the chance to sit in a panel-style, question and answer session where aspiring artists and aspiring industry people could ask any question. The panelists consisted of people from all areas of the music industry—managers, booking agents, A&R reps, artists, even an audio engineer.

About halfway through the forum, someone asked the A&R person for his contact information so they could send him a copy of their demo. He provided his mailing address and then said with a straight face, "And if you can, please send the demo on a Sony type II cassette. Those are the best for recording over." [10]

There was a low hum in the room, sort of like a murmur mixed with the early stages of "booing." No aspiring artist in the room, however, was bold enough to actually commit to the "boo" for fear of offending someone as important as this A&R rep. Nevertheless,

---

[10] Yes, I know I just *dated* myself horribly with that reference to high-quality cassette tapes. Please stop making fun of me and try to focus on the point of this otherwise useful anecdote.

the vibe of the audience shifted a bit from open excitement to the early stages of discouragement.

It was one of those moments where the aspiring industry person in me stood up on the inside with indignation, deeply wounded and wanting to rally against the establishment. How in the world could someone at a major Christian label treat us like that?!

Fast forward fifteen years and some hundreds of demos later and...I have to tell you...in all honesty...I kind of see the A&R guy's point.

All over the country at this very moment, in back closets and spare offices at record companies large and small, there are boxes filled with discarded demo tapes and CDs. It's one of those secrets that all music industry people know, but that aspiring artists never want to believe. The reason is not that record company people are inherently evil. But for some reason, demo tapes are rarely very good.

It has taken me a long time to resign myself to that fact. For years I tried to keep my hopes high, actually taking the time to hand out my business cards at events and investing hours, listening to what had been handed to me by individuals with big dreams and promises that they were my next great artist.

At some point, I had a moment of revelation: Demos can be a wonderfully useful tool, but too often aspiring artists don't know how to use them properly. I have come to believe the greatest value of a demo is *not* the opportunity it gives you to get your music into the right hands. No, the greatest value of a demo is the *developmental opportunity* it provides for the aspiring artist.

With rare exception, prior to recording a demo, most Gospel singers have spent the majority of their performance time in live settings. Whether you were singing in church, at school, or even just in front of your friends and family, you were developing your *live* performance skills.

For many, many aspiring artists, creating a demo is the first time they've had to use their *studio* performance skills. Even if they've had the opportunity to spend time in the studio, singing background vocals or doing overdubs[11] for a church choir album, most people have never had to think of themselves in-studio as the main artist until they decide to create their demo.

Unfortunately, there are few similarities between the skills necessary for effective *live* performance and the skills necessary for effective *studio* performance. As an artist, you will learn the difference by doing both—a lot.

It may be hard to believe that someone who excels at singing in front of people might not have the same degree of excellence behind a studio microphone. To help you to grasp this concept a bit better, I have a question for you: Why do so many of our favorite mainstream artists sound amazing on their CDs and not so amazing when you see them perform live?

Still not convinced? Why do so many mainstream artists choose to lip-sync to tracks when they perform on TV and in live concerts? Trust me. It's not just because of the dancing.

Live performance and studio performance require entirely different skills. And just because you are great at doing one, does not mean you will automatically be great at doing the other.

Don't be deceived. Even if you think you're going to build your career on live recordings, you will still have to know how to deliver in the studio. I am only aware of one major live Gospel CD

---

[11] Overdubs are vocal and instrumental fixes completed in the studio after a live recording.

in the modern era that was sold in stores *without* any overdubs. Let's just say...it wasn't the best decision.

My point is this: In order to be a successful Gospel artist, you will need to have *both* sets of performance skills—live and studio. Creating a demo is an important step in building your studio skills.

If you've not yet had the opportunity to record in a studio as the lead vocalist you may be thinking, "What's so hard about singing in a studio?" Studio singing is difficult for a number of reasons, including these:

- Studio microphones tend to highlight every flaw. They are far less forgiving than live microphones.

- In studio, singers are required to perfect each line, singing the same parts of the song repeatedly. This requires stamina and the ability to recognize your mistakes and correct them.

There are many more differences between studio singing and live singing, which you will learn when you begin working on your own material.

Here are a few suggestions for creating your demo.

Demo Suggestion: Be Wise In Your Song Choices.

One of the most difficult parts about creating a demo is selecting the three to four songs to include. Please keep in mind that a demo is a sample of your material, meant only as an introduction to your talent, therefore, it should not exceed that number of songs. With that in mind, picking the right material is key.

If you are a singer/songwriter, I believe it's important to include songs you've written or co-written. For you, a demo will be a reflection of your writing skills as well as your vocal skills. You will be pitching yourself for consideration as both a singer and a songwriter, so it makes sense to choose material that displays your skill in both of those areas. Rather than picking songs that are your personal favorites, I believe it is important to choose songs that have received the most positive responses during your live performances. Often what actually connects with people is a bit different than what touches us personally. So go with what you know has consistently worked well for you in performance.

For vocalists who do *not* write, the challenge of song choice can be a bit trickier. I would strongly urge you to avoid including songs that have already been made famous by established artists. Sometimes aspiring artists believe the fact that they can sing a Yolanda Adams classic or a Donnie McClurkin hit will be even bigger proof of their talent. In reality, choosing to include a well-known, well-loved song often sets up an unfair comparison that few aspiring artists will be able to work to their advantage.

It is no small feat to sing within Donnie's range or with Yolanda's passion, especially when you do *not* have the advantage of top quality recording facilities. Rather than showcasing your considerable talent, that kind of song choice tends to highlight your weaknesses.

If you aren't fortunate enough to have friends or associates who write, stick to hymns or general worship songs. Again, the main goal will be to find material that has consistently worked well for you with audiences. The more familiar and comfortable you are with the material, the more likely you are to deliver it in-studio with confidence.

Demo Suggestion: Be Careful In Choosing Your Musical Style.

A common mistake I've seen over the years is the aspiring artist who chooses a production style that is a poor fit with the natural style of their voice. Many times I've reviewed demos where the singer has a very traditional voice, but has material consisting of urban or hip-hop tracks. I believe the intent was to demonstrate that the aspiring artist is relevant to youth, or has potential to crossover into the urban marketplace. Unfortunately, the clash of styles demonstrated the exact opposite.

There is no shame at all in having a traditional voice in today's marketplace. If that's the style of music you sing well, the style of your demo should reflect that. Pick traditional material with traditional instrumentation. It will be a stronger demo because it will be better representation of your artistry.

I believe it is always a mistake to attempt to be something other than what you are. Take the time to figure out what you actually do well and then do that thing with confidence. If creating a demo can help you to figure that out, the process has been extremely valuable whether you land a recording deal or not.

Demo Suggestion: Invest In Production Quality.

A key way to make your demo more impressive is to invest in production quality. By production quality I mean the technical elements of your demo, including the equipment used for instrumentation, the studio facilities, and the format on which you store your demo (cassette, DAT, CD, MP3, etc.).

Here's an important piece of advice: Try to avoid thinking, "It's just a demo." Too often when creating a demo, an aspiring artist will slap something together with very little apparent thought or investment. The hope, the expectation is that their enormous potential will outshine a substandard presentation. That kind of thinking can be deadly to your career.

In theory, music industry people, especially A&R reps, *should* have developed the skill to see potential in rough places. In reality, however, that skill is more rare than you think, and often will not be extended to demos from aspiring artists. Again, I do not believe it is because record company people are inherently evil. More likely it is because they are understaffed and overworked.

Let's do the uncomfortable math: There are hundreds of aspiring Gospel artists hoping to get a record deal every year. At the same time, there are only four to five major Gospel labels in business at any one time, each with a maximum roster of twenty to thirty artists, most of whom are currently under long-term contracts. Consider the hours to establish and maintain the careers of the artists who are already under contract, and that leaves a minimum amount of time to scout new talent. To this, let's add the challenges of the current financial climate in the music industry. Total all of those elements and one thing becomes virtually undeniable—record labels are not quite as anxious to find *you* as you are to find them. (Take a deep breath and please try to remember I'm on your side.)

I believe it's necessary to have that picture in the back of your mind, in almost the same way that it's important to find out the weather in a foreign city before you leave for vacation. Knowing the climate tells you what to expect and, more importantly, *how to pack.*

If you know that the most motivated party in the demo pitch is likely to be you, you will hopefully be a bit wiser in how you "pack" that demo. Don't just throw something together as if you were trying to impress your doting grandmother. Nanna may be an easy sell, but a record company won't be quite so generous.

It's not "just a demo." In actuality, it is your one shot to make a statement about who you are as an artist and why a very busy person who has no personal connection to you should stop to pay attention. Don't make them search for the diamond in the rough. Give them something polished and ready that is hard to turn off in the first thirty seconds.

Although no one is expecting you to spend a huge budget on creating a demo, you should be willing to invest in this process. How can you expect a record company to spend hundreds of thousands of dollars on your talent if you are not willing to spend mere hundreds of dollars on yourself?

The good news is that in the modern age of music industry technology, high quality sound is well within your reach. Almost every musician I know—whether amateur or professional—has a basement studio and access to Pro Tools.[12] With that in mind, CD-quality, digital recording has never been more affordable or accessible to the aspiring artist.

If you don't have a friend with a Pro Tools set-up, ask around. Even if no one is willing to donate their services to your venture, you should be able to find a local studio with Pro Tools-quality recording services. Do your research, book some time, and get to work.

---

[12] Pro Tools is a software package used for recording and post-production. It is perhaps the most widely used recording software, and one of the first programs to provide CD-quality recording access on the personal computer.

Demo Suggestion: Put Some Thought Into The Packaging.
It is true that the content of your demo is more important than the packaging. However, when an industry person receives a hundred demos each year, you may need a little help getting yours to stand out. I would encourage you to skip the fancy folders and instead focus on getting a nice head shot (black & white publicity-style photo) and a *brief*—not to exceed 250 words—well-written bio. Anyone considering investing time or money into your talent will need to know how you look and something about your background.

It is surprising how much authenticity and simplicity add class and professionalism to a well-crafted demo. Don't hype yourself beyond what's reasonable. State the facts about your background and experience and let it go. Veteran music industry people can see right through the fluff, so do yourself a favor and leave that stuff out.

Finally, I would *not* suggest spending a lot of money on your packaging. Your resources are valuable and, even under the best conditions, the package is likely to end up in one of those boxes in the spare office.

That may be an uncomfortable reality, but there's no need to be offended. Even if the company was still around, I doubt that anyone at Benson would know where Fred Hammond's solo demo is right now. That doesn't take away from the fact that he landed a deal with that company and went on to become one of the top-selling artists of his generation. So, relax friend. Keep your eyes on the goal.

Demo Suggestion: Do Your Research.
Before you send out a demo, take the time to determine if the places where you are planning to send it have a demo policy.

Today, many record companies will refuse any demo they have not specifically requested. That kind of policy is called a "no unsolicited demo" rule.

It may seem unfair, but the policy exists mainly because of time constraints and a history of low quality demos. When most Gospel record companies are severely understaffed, it is not a good use of company resources to spend the time that would be necessary receiving, opening, listening, and responding to a regular stream of unsolicited demos.

There are few ways to counter this policy, but all is not lost. If you spend the time doing the things we've discussed over the past twenty pages or so, you will inevitably begin to build relationships with key people. And there is nothing wrong with asking permission to send a demo to someone you've met or spoken with before. If they've seen you perform live, or met you at an industry conference or ministry event, they are more likely to say yes, and more likely to actually listen to your demo when you send it.

Relationships like that offer an added bonus. Even if you don't land a deal, you are likely to get feedback from someone with real experience. Since development should be your primary focus at this point in your career, that kind of input is simply invaluable.

A Few Final Thoughts...

You will probably only get *one shot* at sending your demo to someone. Demos are not something you will be invited to update and re-send to people of influence every few months. More likely, for the people who receive your demo, this will be the only impression they will have of your artistry.

As scary as that may sound, there's no need for you to pressure yourself and there's certainly no need to rush. When you embrace the process of demo creation as a useful and important step in your artistic development, you will lose some of the urgency to finish it.

Instead of focusing on simply getting a demo out there, use this opportunity to put some thought into how your artistry and ministry will transfer to a recorded project. If someone never had the chance to see you live and knew very little about you, what would you want them to hear?

Take the time to make the best demo you can. It doesn't have to be perfect. However, it should be an accurate representation of your ability at a level of quality someone could appreciate—even if that person wasn't a close friend or relative.

The Value Of A Record Deal

It is safe to say that the end goal for most aspiring artists is to land a deal, an exclusive recording contract, with a major record label. Today, if you were to walk into a room full of singers and offer any of them a recording contract, a vast majority would jump at the chance and happily consider that moment their big break.

In fact, that promise is the reason why year after year singers are willing to line up for hours—sometimes days—in major cities across the country to audition for *American Idol*. The exposure on television is exciting, and the chance to work with established music industry personalities may be nice, but the ultimate goal is to win that top spot and be signed to a record deal with a major label.

The dream is shared by so many singers, regardless of their stage of development, that *American Idol* is not only one of the top-rated shows in the United States, but versions of the show exist in almost every major country. In addition, the concept of *American Idol* has been reshaped a dozen ways to create versions specific to other genres of music, including country and Gospel.

Ironically, if you were to ask most of those same aspiring artists why a record deal was so important or exactly what is involved in a recording contract, they probably couldn't offer a concrete reason. They might talk about the lifelong dream of seeing their face on a CD, appearing in their very own video, or having a system to launch them into international stardom. Those singers with a bit more experience might mention the draw of a large signing bonus and the opportunity to finally pursue their music full-time.

All of those notions are heartfelt elements of the dream. Unfortunately, the reality is often quite different.

Don't panic. It is not my goal to dash your dreams. Instead, I'd like to offer a more useful concept. A recording contract can be a valuable tool, when viewed from the proper perspective. To do that, I think it's important to take a look back.

Historically Speaking

I believe the modern, *American Idol* notion of the record deal has its roots in the hey-day of pop music, the 1960s. Back then, companies like Motown Records built their legend by taking raw, working talent and sending it through the star machine.

Theirs was a world where the record company was not just talent scout, booking agent, and radio promoter, it was also publisher, studio, tour promoter, choreographer, media trainer, and stylist. Raw talent went in and stars came out.

I'm sure the reality felt quite different to the Motown acts and to the executives in charge. The singers worked long, hard hours in-studio and longer, harder days on the road. And Motown founder, Berry Gordy, said, "Motown was built on the idea that there was only one way to survive—single by single, song by song, hit by hit."[13] Clearly what the public came to embrace as magical was truly the result of years of hard work.

---

[13] Dahl, Bill and Keith Hughes. "The Complete Motown Singles Volume I: 1959–1961." Hip-O Select. Motown 2004.

When I use the term "star machine," I'm really talking about artist development. Motown was a hub of artist development—discovering artists, training them, sustaining them. Berry Gordy was hands-on as a business man, but he was also hands-on as a songwriter, producer, manager, and radio promoter. He and the team he built made it their goal to develop successful artistry by working every aspect of an artist's career.

Perhaps because that period in popular music history marked the first generation of artists to use television as a key outlet for exposure, the notion of the star machine became thoroughly imbedded in the American consciousness. Whatever the cause, it is a notion that survives, while the reality of the music business has evolved several times since then.

Now that we've taken a glance back, let's talk about more recent developments.

After The Star Machine

The evolution of the music industry—the ways in which the business of making and selling music has changed over the past fifty years—will have serious implications for anyone aspiring to make a living in the current marketplace. Ironically, because the music industry *seems* to be so visible to the general public, most aspiring artists and musicians think they understand more about it than they actually do.

More than 30 million people watch *American Idol* each week and just think of the millions who spend hours every day watching MTV, VH-1, and BET. The music industry, along with the artists and products it generates, has unfolded before us in living color for more than twenty-five years. And in the age of reality shows like "Making

The Band," now more than ever, the general public believes it has been an up-close witness to the everyday world of the music industry.

In some ways, the American public *is* more informed. Today, almost anyone could name two or three of the top music producers and maybe even one major record label president. I'm not sure that could have been said in the 1970s. However, knowing the names is a far cry from understanding the roles and manner in which all of the parts work together.

Many a bad recording contract has been signed as a result of misperceptions. So for you, understanding the core realities of the music industry is important. Your success will depend upon you having a proper concept.

Outside of TV reality shows, the star machine no longer exists. In fact, it is highly unlikely today, especially in Gospel music, that an aspiring singer would be signed to a major label deal without previous experience, and without having done his fair share of work in all of the areas we discussed in the last section (see "Necessary Elements").

With that in mind, what exactly is the value of a recording contract? As we'll see shortly, the answer to that question is changing even as we speak. Nevertheless, I'd like to offer you a basic concept that has been in place functionally for at least the past twenty years.

When an aspiring artist signs a recording contract with a major label, he is promising to deliver his talent, name, likeness, and often his songwriting interest in exchange for money to create album projects and a good faith promise from that record company to vigorously promote and market those albums.

A detailed examination of the structure and meaning of record-ing contracts is beyond the scope of this handbook. Nevertheless, let's look at the basic paradigm for record deals.

In general, a record company provides:

- Money to record and manufacture your CDs
- Money to promote and market your CDs
- Photos and marketing materials
- Representation and promotion with national radio
- Representation and publicity with national media (TV, print, Internet)
- Distribution of your CDs to retailers
- A percentage of income based upon sales of your CDs (royalty)

Typically, in exchange, the artist grants to the record company:

- *Exclusive* use of his musical talent
- Use of his name
- Use of his likeness (image)
- His songwriting interest (publishing)
- Ownership of the recorded songs (masters)
- A specified number of album projects

Those are the basic elements of the relationship between a major label and artist. The regulation of those basic elements is normally outlined within the **exclusive artist agreement**, which can run more than one hundred pages in length and cover everything from artist appearances on other albums to payments for new forms of music technology.[14]

---

[14] Because new technology tends to emerge every fifteen years or so and change the dominant format for commercial music, artist agreements normally include language that governs the manner in which those new formats are handled. Over the past thirty years alone, we've witnessed the transition from LP to 8-track tape to cassette tape to CD to MP3.

For most artists, contractual language is overwhelming, and the concepts may seem outrageous, particularly when you just want to sing. But careful consideration and negotiation of the elements of the agreement—preferably with the assistance of competent legal counsel—will mean the difference between taking your career to that long-awaited next level and being stuck in a bad business relationship from which your career may never fully recover.

Throughout our conversation so far, I've reiterated the fact that the Gospel music marketplace—as a unique division of the overall music industry—mirrors the mainstream marketplace in many ways. In the area of recording contracts, the Gospel industry takes its cues almost entirely from the mainstream world, with several key differences. Among those differences are:

- The size (amount) of artist advances
- The size (amount) of recording budgets
- The term of the agreement (number of album projects)
- The size (amount) of artist and producer royalties

Quite simply, the Gospel music marketplace is smaller—in both audience size and annual revenue—than the mainstream marketplace. Therefore, the finances involved in a Gospel artist recording agreement will be in keeping with that smaller marketplace. In other words, there is less money to be made in Gospel, so there will be less money paid to the Gospel artist than to his mainstream counterpart in virtually every area of a recording contract.

On the surface, that fact may seem disheartening. However, when you understand issues of **recoupment**, the smaller scale can be somewhat beneficial to a Gospel artist. The less money you see up front, the more likely you are to actually receive earnings from sales of your CD.

Recoupment, one of the biggest buzz-words in any recording agreement, is also the least generally understood. Perhaps the simplest way to understand the concept is to think of payments to an artist as an interest-free loan. Each dollar paid to the artist will be paid back to the record company through sales of that artist's products (CDs, DVDs, etc.). In most cases, nothing you will earn in a recording agreement will be given freely. You will have to pay it all back. The manner in which you will pay it back—at what rate, on which items, and over what time period—will be one of the most important parts of your contract negotiation.

When an artist has earned back all of the money paid to him (or paid on his behalf) over a set period of time or in connection with a specific project, he is said to be **recouped**. When an artist has *not* earned back the money paid to him (or paid on his behalf) over a set period of time or in connection with a specific project, he is said to be **unrecouped**.

The issue of recoupment is important because, with rare exception, an artist will not begin to receive actual money in connection with the sales of his CDs or DVDs until he has earned back the costs to make that project. You will begin to receive actual checks from sales of your CD only when you are recouped.

Here's a very brief, very basic illustration based upon real-world numbers for a first-time Gospel artist agreement:

In general, an artist will recoup his costs at the artist royalty rate specified in his recording agreement. Let's say that royalty rate is 12%. That would mean the artist would earn 12% of the wholesale price of each CD.[15] If that wholesale price is $10, the artist would earn $1.20 per CD sold.

Therefore, if an album cost $65,000 to create, the artist will earn back that $65,000 at the rate of $1.20 per CD. At that rate, assuming no other contractual complications, the artist would begin to receive checks for his artist royalties after he has sold more than 54,000 copies of his CD.

Now, I have simplified this example for ease of explanation. In reality, many other issues would come into play, including concepts like packaging deductions, cross-collateralization, all-in producer royalties, recoupable marketing costs, recoupable advances, etc. Recording agreements are **not** easy. You will likely never master them or feel entirely comfortable with them.

Don't feel bad. Recording contracts are hard for every artist, no matter how long they've been in the industry. Therefore, do yourself a favor and begin doing some research on good entertainment lawyers *with experience in the Gospel marketplace*.[16] You will need one to help you to make the best deal you can.

I have taken the time to discuss the issue of recoupment to create a bit of perspective for you. Considering the scale of our marketplace, I don't believe it's helpful to see a big payday as your *primary* reason for wanting a recording contract. In reality, due to the complexities of recording agreements, and the smaller scale of the Gospel music marketplace, most Gospel artists do *not* receive real income from their artist royalties.

---

[15] The wholesale price is the price at which record companies sell your CDs to retailers (Best Buy, Wal-Mart, Lifeway, etc). Since retailers need to make a profit, the price we pay for a CD in a store or on-line is always marked up.

[16] One easy way to begin that research is by reading CD credits. Artists often thank their lawyers in their album notes.

In fact, the best way to ensure income from your album sales is to diversify your artistry by also becoming a songwriter or producer. Because payment of songwriter royalties is regulated by Federal law, generally a record company must pay a songwriter in connection with CD sales beginning with the sale of the very first CD.[17]

Producer royalties are not quite so cut-and-dried. However, because record companies must pay a fund[18] to a producer to actually make a recording, generally producers see money long before a CD hits stores. Although any *royalties* would have to wait until costs have been recouped, a producer is likely to receive at least a portion of his fees upfront.

In light of those things, an artist who is also a songwriter and/or producer would have multiple streams of income from his CD projects. He would also be likely to actually receive money from the sales of his CDs *prior* to recoupment.

Truth be told, that important fact is one of the reasons why so many artists—Gospel and mainstream—write and produce their own material. The opportunity to increase your potential earnings from your CD and DVD sales is a powerful draw.

Nevertheless, I must caution you: It is a terrible mistake to pursue songwriting and/or production simply to diversify your earnings from your own projects. It is better to record great songs and to work with excellent producers than to do everything yourself. Ultimately, the higher quality your CD, the more copies you are likely to sell. And we all know a small percentage of *something* is better than a big percentage of *nothing*.

---

[17] There are always exceptions. In cases where an artist agreement has a publishing component, and the artist receives publishing advances, recoupment would again apply.

[18] A producer fund is *an* approved budget outlining the costs to create the songs. It typically includes hard costs as well as a fee for the producer's services.

So focus on making the best album projects you can. If your songwriting and production skills grow to accommodate that level of excellence, that's great. If not, be honest enough with yourself to prefer outside material. Ultimately your CDs will be stronger, and you will be more likely to retain your recording contract.

Now that we have a working concept of the most basic relationship between a record company and an artist, I believe we're finally ready to talk about the real value of a record deal.

The Advantages Of Having A Record Deal

From outside of the music industry looking in, it's easy to see why so many people believe that if they can sing, they *should* become a recording artist. It seems to be the logical next step, like going to medical school if you wanted to become a doctor.

As we've already seen, the mainstream media offer a powerful, but very limited perspective of the music industry. Consequently, most aspiring artists today have a faulty paradigm of the dream. I believe that can be especially true in Gospel music.

In my years of speaking with aspiring Gospel artists, the majority of the questions I've received have revolved around how to get a record deal. Yet in those same conversations, it became clear that very few of those individuals had ever stopped to consider if getting a record deal was indeed the best way to accomplish their goals.

In reality, a recording contract will be truly beneficial to a small percentage of aspiring artists only. For the majority, other options—some of which we will discuss shortly—may, in fact, be more beneficial. It may seem hard to believe, but knowing which road *not* to take is often more important than knowing which road to take.

We have now dedicated several pages to the relationship between a record company and an artist. It's extremely important to know the basics of that interaction in order to lay a proper foundation moving forward.

Despite its length, a recording agreement makes no guarantees of success. During my years in this industry, I have yet to see an artist agreement that stipulates the *manner* in which a record company will promote an artist's albums, or that defines the roles and obligations of the record label staff.

A recording contract may outline the very intricate formulas for payments and recoupment, but what it *won't* do is promise to make you a star. Nobody can make that guarantee. Nevertheless, if we look at a recording contract as a *special tool for a specific stage in the development of your artistry and ministry*, we will be able to gain a clearer understanding of the value of that tool.

Having a record deal *will not guarantee* you any of the following:

- A #1 record
- Billing on a major tour
- Booking on major TV shows
- Award nominations

You may indeed be blessed to accomplish those things as a result of having a record deal. Unfortunately, you are also likely to release your CD and find that those milestones remain outside of your grasp. The reason is simple: The marketing and promotion of a CD, despite certain industry-wide norms, are *not exact sciences*.

Hopefully your record company will put their full efforts behind your CD and look for innovative ways to promote your artistry. But even under the best circumstances, there is no way to ensure that your project will outsell expectations or connect with people in a commercially profound way.

I have not said those things to discourage you. On the contrary, my goal is to properly align your expectations. If you approach the issue of landing a record deal as if it will be the missing link to stardom, you will severely limit your opportunities for success. In truth, a record deal is an important tool for the pivotal moment when you launch your ministry on a national level. When you learn to see a deal in that light, it will become easier for you to evaluate your opportunities more accurately and to make better choices.

A record deal can be an important tool in the advancement of your artistry, but not for the reasons most people expect. Rather than a ticket to instant celebrity, a recording contract with a major label is likely to give you three basic things:

- Funding
- Credibility
- Access

Let's take a very brief look at each area.

Benefit #1: Funding

One of the most important provisions in a recording contract is money to record and manufacture your CD and DVD projects. Although you will have to earn it back through the process of recoupment, there is great benefit to having a business partner who will provide all of the upfront capital for your vision.

CD production in Gospel music will generally cost $50,000–$400,000 (for items including studio time and materials, producer fees, musician and vocalist salaries, travel, lodging, advances, union fees, and mastering). Marketing and promotion on a major Gospel release can cost $60,000–$500,000 (for services and items including creation and design of CD packaging, marketing materials, advertising, events, and radio and media servicing).

Imagine how long it would take and how difficult it would be if you had to earn or raise that kind of money on your own.

Although it is certainly possible to create a CD for far less money independently, most artists will not have access to the same level of production on their own as they would with a major label backing them. It would be difficult to get the highest quality producers, musicians, vocalists, engineers, and studios at significantly discounted prices without some heavy-duty relationships. As for marketing and promotion, it is almost impossible to get around the hard costs of advertising, retail programs, and national promotion and publicity campaigns. Those costs are not normally reduced for independent artists.

Benefit #2: Credibility

Today, there are easily more aspiring and developing artists competing for the attention of audiences and industry tastemakers than at any point in music history. Just take a look at the number of music pages on MySpace alone and you'll see what I mean.

One big way for you to distinguish yourself among that crowd is to have the backing of a major label. A record deal with a successful label means that you are instantly associated with an established brand. Audiences and gatekeepers at major media outlets may not yet know *you*, but when they see your name and image accompanied by the familiar logo of a record label, it helps them to identify you. It adds legitimacy to your artistry. Quite frankly you are able to lean on the strength of an established brand, while you are working to develop your career.

Benefit #3: Access

There are many doors that simply will not open to unsigned or independent artists. Ask anyone who has taken the courageous step to release an independent CD and they will tell you how difficult it is—even in Gospel music—to get airplay on major radio stations. The same challenge often applies to receiving coverage from major media outlets. The biggest door of all—national retail—can be almost impossible to crack without a system behind you.

Having a deal with a major label tends to open all of those doors. If a company has had success with other artists, or currently has major names on their roster, they should be able to walk your project into the door on the strength of their reputation. Those relationships at key radio, media, and retail outlets are simply one of the most valuable assets of a major label deal.

Funding, credibility, and **access** may not be exciting buzz words. I'm sure they pale in comparison to the notion of a #1 record or Grammy nomination. Nevertheless, they are vital needs for anyone pursuing national artistry.

To Sign Or Not To Sign

Earlier in our discussion, I said the ultimate goals of Gospel music are to spread the message of the Gospel of Jesus Christ, to be an expression of worship to God and to bring hope and encouragement to believers. It is important to realize that a Gospel artist is fully capable of accomplishing those goals *without ever* having a record deal.

Because the Church Community is a key part of the overall Gospel marketplace, there are abundant opportunities for an artist to regularly perform and sell his own music without the assistance of a record company. With that in mind, and in light of the complications and legal restrictions that will inevitably come with a recording contract, it is important to give careful consideration to this issue: Should you seek a recording contract and if so, when?

While I cannot give you a step-by-step guide to answering those questions, I can offer you some keys to consider. **A recording contract with a major label will be *of greatest value* to aspiring Gospel artists who meet the following criteria:**

- The artist possesses all or most of the "necessary elements"
- The artist is plugged into and active in a local ministry
- The artist is performing regionally and nationally on a *regular* basis
- The artist has considerable experience performing in-studio

The biggest mistake most aspiring artists make is believing that a deal with a record label will give you the keys I've just listed. It is vital to recognize that in Gospel music a recording deal *does not initiate* your career and ministry. Instead, it should merely be a catalyst to launch your career and ministry to a national level. Therefore, to ensure the greatest opportunity for success from a recording contract, you need to complete a good deal of developmental legwork in advance.

Let's think of it this way: An athlete does not *begin* his career at the Olympics. The Olympics may bring him to international attention, but they will always be the culmination of years of training and effort. There is no getting around it. To be properly equipped to participate within a national and international arena, you have to do your homework.

Regarding the issue of *when* to look for a record deal...As we all know, timing is everything. In reality, if you have done the work to meet all or most of the criteria above, it will become pretty obvious to you when you are ready for a recording contract with a major label. The need for a ministry tool—a piece of product (CD or DVD) to sell after your performances—can be an indicator. Another big indicator may be the realization that you have maximized your efforts in all of the key areas—live performances, radio and media exposure, and studio production. If you've developed *beyond your circle of influence*, it may be time to take that next leap.

I know this can be a lot of information to digest. I would urge you to take some real time to contemplate the information in this section for the aspiring artist, particularly our discussion on necessary elements. Jot down notes and thoughts about your development and vision and reevaluate your answers over time, as you grow creatively and in ministry.

Please keep in mind, the best gift you can give yourself in this process is *honesty*. The goal is to become exactly who **you** *were created to be*. With that in mind, there is no shame in honest evaluation of your artistry and ministry, even if that evaluation results in reshaping your dream.

It is better to be truthful in private and have the opportunity to correct your course, than to walk out the results of your errors in a public forum. The bargain CD bins are full of artists who failed to ask themselves the right questions at the right times.

The most important thing to remember about the process we've been discussing is that it requires *you* to make the first and most continuous commitment to your artistry and ministry. If you are faithful in developing yourself, opportunities have a wonderful way of finding you.

Whenever I share that piece of information, I tend to see a glazey look come over the eyes of the aspiring artists in the room. For some reason, people seem to prefer the notion of meeting that key industry person or the fantasy of being signed instantly after giving an impromptu performance to an established artist.[19] But the reality of becoming the best artist and most effective minister you can be should excite you more.

There are few things more fulfilling than catching a vision from God, working with the help of the Holy Spirit to build that vision and realizing the fruit of your efforts—especially if you can impact people's lives in the process. There is joy in the journey, my friend. Please avoid the very human impulse to find shortcuts.

If you've made that commitment to your ministry, and you are convinced yours is a call to national artistry, then a record deal with a major label may be a necessary tool for you.

Choosing The Right Record Company

If we were having a discussion about finding a mate, it would be easy for us to agree that limiting your search to the best looking or richest people is probably not the wisest way to choose a husband or wife. The most important criteria is compatibility.

---

[19] A la Boyz II Men and Michael Bivens (a member of New Edition) in the early '90s. The story goes that four young men from Philly gave an on-the-spot, a cappella performance to Michael Bivens after a New Edition concert one night. Bivens was so impressed that he signed the group to a deal. That group became Boyz II Men. The rest is music history.

I believe that same concept applies to choosing a record company. The biggest mistake you could make is to limit your consideration to the biggest record company. Just because a particular label has the most artists or the most #1 albums does not mean that company would be the best home for your artistry and ministry. Your goal should be to find a record company that is compatible with your vision and best able to meet the needs of your current stage of artistry, while offering you growth potential.

You need to know, regardless of their success, not every record label excels at every form of music. More importantly, not every label excels at launching developing artists.

To avoid persuading you toward any particular brand, and in light of the huge transitions currently happening in the music industry, I have chosen not to list Gospel record companies by name. I would encourage you to do your research. Refer to the trade magazines and sourcebooks we've discussed and look at the information on the CDs in your music collection.

As you look at the different companies, don't just look at the names on their roster (list of signed artists). Look at *when*—at what stage in their careers—that company signed those particular artists. Here's the reason: The needs of established artists are far different from those of developing or first-time artists. Therefore a label that has a history of success with established artists, but not as strong a history with launching new artists, may not be the best fit for you right now.

One of the advantages of attending music conferences and major industry events is the opportunity it gives you to learn about record companies. For most labels, national industry conventions are important branding opportunities where they present showcases and have booths featuring information about their company, their artists and their upcoming releases. In addition, many times key record label executives and staff members attend those events, participating in panel discussions and leading workshops.

Although labels may not be scouting new talent at those events, it is an excellent opportunity for you to become more familiar with the differences between the labels, their rosters, and their key players. Take advantages of opportunities like that to do your homework.

The moment when you actually have an offer from a label is not the time to cram. Rather, an informed negotiation should be your goal. Although you should have help from competent legal counsel, it is up to *you* to have a sense of your artistry along with the goals of your ministry. That knowledge of self along with the research you've gathered on the label will enable you to distinguish better between a record company that is a good fit and one that is not.

Before we end this section, I'd like to make one final note regarding record deals.

The record company is an important piece of the puzzle, but you must never forget it is only one piece. Realizing your full potential will require the ongoing efforts of you and your team (management, booking agency, attorney, etc.).

The right deal may help you to achieve the next level, but staying on that level and expanding your goals will be the result of your ongoing commitment to your calling. Even the most successful artist under the very best circumstances will need to continue working to hone his craft and further connecting with his audience in order to maintain that success.

Part Three:
For The Aspiring Industry Executive

The Call To Industry

Not all of us who feel a pull toward the Gospel music industry are called to be artists, songwriters, or producers. Those roles in the industry may be the most public, but there are many other ways to earn a living in this business. More importantly, there are many ways to be of service in the Gospel music marketplace apart from creating or performing music.

Use your imagination for a moment to see a room containing 100 people. Let's pretend that group of people represents the entire population of both the Creative and Business Communities of the Gospel music industry. Within that room, artists, songwriters, and producers would make up about fifteen of those people while the remaining eighty-five people would be members of the Business Community.

Just open the booklet of any CD, and it should become instantly clear that for every face on a CD cover there are dozens and sometimes hundreds of people who contribute to, support, and service that artist's career. Those people may not be celebrities to the fans, but to an artist who is well-served by their efforts, those people are essential and priceless.

When I first began to consider a career in the Gospel music world, I certainly had no concept of that reality. Because I was an avid reader of album packaging, I could recognize the names I saw again and again inside the liner notes of my cassettes and CDs, but I didn't know what an A&R representative was, or what an executive producer did. I knew that some of my favorite artists took the time to thank radio announcers and retailers, but I had no sense of their role in the process.

To recap from earlier in our discussion, the Business Community consists of:

- Record companies
- Managers/Booking Agents
- Radio
- Media (TV, print, Internet)
- Promoters (live performances)
- Retail (sales outlets)

We've already discussed the basic ways in which those people interact with the Creative Community. It is important for aspiring artists to have that basic knowledge of the parts, in order to understand the process happening around them once they finally have a CD in release. For those of you who feel a pull to the Business Community, I'd like to offer a more complete overview.

Similar to artistry, there is no surefire set of rules for breaking into the industry side of the music business. Depending on where within the Business Community your interest lies, there are numerous ways to get your foot in the door and begin to gain valuable experience. And because most industry jobs are housed within the corporate world, many of the simple strategies and skills for getting a job in any industry—investing in your education, developing interview skills, building a résumé, etc.—will help you land at least an entry level position in almost any segment of the music Business Community.

It may surprise you to learn that most record companies have the same basic structure as any other type of corporation. While A&R, marketing, publicity, and promotions may be hallmarks of the record label world, divisions within any major label would also include auxiliary departments such as accounting, business affairs (legal), human resources, maintenance, and the mailroom. Jobs within those departments are normally open to anyone, not just people with aspirations toward other music industry interests.

When I landed my first job at a record label, I was surprised to find that many of the people who were valuable and long-time employees of the company considered their jobs to be like any other nine-to-five employment. Of course, there were the uncommon perks of free CDs, access to concert tickets, and the occasional sighting of a well-known artist waiting for the elevator.

For the most part, however, the employees in the auxiliary departments of the label were not simply biding their time while waiting for a spot to open up in A&R or Marketing. They were good at what they did and remained at the company for the same reason you would work anywhere—benefits, a pleasant corporate environment, steady income, opportunities for growth, and the chance to develop new skills.

Chances are, if you have taken the time to purchase and read this book, you are *not* planning to make your career in one of the auxiliary departments at a record label. Nevertheless, I think it's important to provide that context because aspiring industry people can suffer from many of the same misperceptions that plague aspiring artists. The media reflects a very limited view of the music world, therefore, we become limited in our concepts.

Unfortunately, I have learned that people with limited concepts become the dreamers of misguided dreams.

I heard a sermon many years ago where the speaker, Richard Foth, said, "We serve a God who dreams big dreams for us." I have come to embrace that thought over the course of my career and ministry. And the more that idea has become alive to me, the more phenomenal doors God has been able to walk me through.

I believe He wants to be the same God to you. But first we need to broaden a few limited concepts. The best place to begin that part of our discussion is with a story that is close to my heart.

My Story (The Beginning)

My call to the Gospel music industry came quite unexpectedly. It began as a simple burden for Gospel artists that I became aware of midway through my time in journalism school.

I have spent the majority of my life deeply in love with Gospel music and intrigued by the details surrounding my favorite artists and albums. In my pre-teen years, the desire to keep up with album releases, artists, and concerts in my area became more than a pastime.

By the fall of 1990 when I entered graduate school, the faces on my CDs had become real people to me. Rather than distant celebrities, I had come to view them as men and women of God who had been such a blessing to me with their music that I began lifting them up to the Lord in my personal prayer time. In fact, in the year before I was hired for my first industry job, there were many days I would pull out my CD case and intercede for the artists represented there as if I knew them.

Around that time something strange happened—my focus began to shift from that of a **fan** to that of a **servant**.

During my college years, I had become a regular concertgoer. However, at that pivotal season, when I would arrive at a concert the Holy Spirit would say very clearly to me, "You know you're here to serve, right?" I was not in the habit of hearing from the Lord in such a personal way, so I took the impulse quite seriously.

Now, money is scarce for most college students. So it is more than a bit challenging to spend $15 or $20 on a concert ticket, wait in a long line to get in and then hear God tell you that you cannot simply sit and enjoy the show! Nevertheless, I obeyed.

I would go to the nearest artist product table and ask the person there if they needed any help folding T-shirts or counting CDs. Normally that person would be someone traveling with the artist, but occasionally it was the artist himself. I didn't know it at the time, but most developing artists are chronically understaffed, so the answer was almost always an enthusiastic "yes!"

I'd like to tell you that in my wisdom and ability to strategize, I saw this as a stepping stone to something. In fact, I did not. My only intention was to obey what I heard from the Lord and offer the best service I could. I didn't know anything about the Gospel music industry, but I knew how to count and how to fold.

After several such experiences, I discovered that the people behind the table would talk to me. And as I listened and humbly served, the Lord would provide opportunities for me to ask questions. I never asked them to *do* anything for me. I simply shared a few things I thought God was saying about where He was leading me.

The things I learned during those conversations were rarely quick fixes. No one offered me a job. But each conversation gave me a bit of information I didn't have before. As I took those tidbits back to my prayer closet over the next year, God began to prepare my heart for my career.

Often when I receive questions from aspiring industry executives, the focus is on networking or showing how much they already know. However, over the years I've seen that most first chances—whether internships, first jobs, or simply first audiences with people of influence—come as the result of a key person sensing your attitude, the focus of your heart.

If my *primary* goal at that time had been to simply pursue a career in Gospel music, I would have done things differently. Perhaps I would have dropped out of journalism school and tried to get a music business degree. I certainly would have been more direct in my conversations with the industry people I met at those concerts.

Had my focus been purely on networking, sharing my dreams with key people, or seeing what someone could do for *me*, I would surely have approached each of those opportunities with a more self-serving mindset.

I cannot tell you it's wrong to pursue your dreams strategically, but I can tell you that approach would have severely limited my future. Let me explain.

Although I sensed a call from the Lord, I knew very little about the marketplace where He was leading me. I had certain factual knowledge about Gospel music, but I had no real-world experience and I had no concept of how the industry worked. Therefore, to develop or pursue a strategy based on the limited knowledge I had wouldn't have gotten me very far.

My goal at the time was not to land a job, but simply to be obedient to God and serve wherever I could. Consequently, my posture was that of a giver rather than that of a receiver. As a result, I believe the industry people I met sensed a sincerity that made them comfortable speaking openly with me. Even better, because that approach was rare, it made them remember me.

Toward the end of my time in graduate school, a person I'd spoken with at one of those tables called me to tell me Fred

Hammond was starting a production company and that he was looking for employees. The young man thought of me and gave me a heads up. The connection with Fred wasn't made immediately, but a door was opened that led to my first industry job.

I have come to believe that God took me through a rather unconventional route to teach me some principles I could not have learned any other way. Not everyone will enter this industry in the manner I did. But I would encourage those of you who want to work in the Business Community of Gospel music to embrace three keys:

- Build a strong spiritual foundation
- Develop a compassion for artists
- Maintain a willingness to serve

In the more than fifteen years since that season in my life, those three keys have remained the foundation for every opportunity I've gotten and have made all the difference in my results. Rather than simply working a series of music industry jobs, I've been able to serve some of the most amazingly talented people in a variety of positions, while developing relationships that lasted beyond any individual project. I have also been able to learn *life* lessons—not just work lessons—while building an impressive résumé.

My strategies were not the key to those opened doors. In fact, my limited perspective would have led me toward an entirely different goal.

If you had asked me in the summer of 1991 what I thought God meant by pulling me toward the Gospel music industry, I would have told you that He wanted me to become a publicist. Since my background was in journalism and I was an aspiring writer, that was the only logical conclusion. My interpretation of God's direction would have been based upon my very limited perspective.

But by opening my heart to His will over my aspirations and by maintaining humility in service, I cleared the way for God to give me something much broader. I have been honored over the years to hold positions not just as a publicist but also as a radio promoter, A&R director, and artist manager all while working on some of the most significant Gospel music projects of this era.

I took the risk to exchange my limited knowledge for God's unlimited wisdom, and He strategically unfolded a career that surpassed my dreams. Throughout it all, my strategy has remained the same—to be obedient to God and serve wherever He leads me.

Before we move on to a few pieces of practical advice, let's take a closer look at the three keys I mentioned.

Key #1: A Strong Spiritual Foundation

For many of us, it may be easy to understand why spiritual matters should remain at the core of an *artist's* life. If an individual is going to write, record, and perform Gospel music there is a basic expectation that he should be well-versed in spiritual matters and (hopefully) consistent in his lifestyle.

It may be more difficult to understand why a spiritual foundation should be necessary for an industry executive. Putting aside matters of theology, I have always believed that if a person is going to pursue any career field, he should be as well-versed as possible in that field. True success will always be based upon how well you've done your homework.

Before you enter this industry, you need to know this: For most Gospel artists and Gospel music consumers (fans), the music is core to their lifestyle. The majority of Gospel artists grew up in church, learned to sing or play in church, and will give the majority of their performances in church settings. Likewise, a large percentage of Gospel music consumers are regular churchgoers who incorporate Gospel music into their lifestyles.

With those things in mind, the serious business person should realize that if both the producers and consumers of your product come from the same unique culture, the degree to which you understand and connect with that culture will in large part determine your level of success. *To put it more simply:* If you do not speak the language of your artists and the language of your consumers, it will be difficult to meet their needs.

That business concept is not unique to the world of Gospel music. While the operative "culture" in the Gospel music marketplace may be the church, there are many other musical genres to which that concept would apply. Anyone who has ever worked in country music, jazz, or hip-hop, could tell you how important it is to understand and embrace the "culture" of those individual marketplaces in order to be successful. In those marketplaces, as within Gospel music, the issue of *authenticity* is essential to the artists and the fans.

I've found that in the world of Gospel music your authenticity as a professional will be felt by artists and will influence their level of comfort in working with you. Likewise, in your interactions with the wider industry community—particularly the Church Community—the level of commitment and cooperation you receive will be strongly influenced by your perceived authenticity.

But what determines your authenticity?

I believe a person's authenticity will be largely determined by his core values, his foundation. You can study a culture and learn the language of the people within that culture, but if you do not truly understand and embrace the values of that culture it is nearly impossible to be viewed as genuine by the natives.

Now let's apply that concept to Gospel music:

There is no easy way around it. Gospel music is founded mainly within the culture of the church. Gospel music is firmly rooted in Christian beliefs and draws heavily from the content and concepts of the Bible. Furthermore, a large percentage of Gospel artists are also ministers or pastors.

To work closely with Gospel artists, it may not be essential to share their specific doctrinal beliefs. However, I believe it is difficult to maximize your efforts in this marketplace without having a strong personal faith as your foundation.

I use the word "foundation" because I believe our faith should be just that. It should be the base upon which the rest of our efforts will be built. It should be the primary thing that guides us and informs our perspective.

For those of us in the Business Community, a strong spiritual foundation is essential because we are the bridge between the creative and the commercial aspects of Gospel music. Whether we work in A&R, radio promotions, marketing, management, or retail, the burden will often fall upon us to translate the artistic and spiritual aspects of Gospel music into the language of commerce.

In my career, to accomplish my corporate tasks and still promote and protect the artistic vision of my artists, it was not enough to simply be *familiar* with both languages. I had to become *fluent* in corporate matters while maintaining my fluency in spiritual matters. The corporate matters could be taught through my work experience; however, the spiritual matters required me to draw from—and continue to develop—my foundation of faith.

I could learn administrative procedure, A&R protocol, and the art of maintaining a production budget. At times it was challenging to master those corporate skills, but they could certainly be taught within the context of my work experience. It was another matter entirely to know how to understand and pray for the spiritual needs of my artists and producers, particularly when I was on deadline to deliver a CD. Over the course of my career, those moments happened more frequently than you might guess.

I know of no shortcut to building that kind of foundation. However, I would encourage you to view your relationship with God as the central aspect of your life. Invest in your own spiritual growth with the same enthusiasm and focus that you would commit to your education or professional development. Ultimately you will be better equipped for the road ahead.

Key #2: Compassion For Artists

Earlier I mentioned that a byproduct of my commitment to pray for my favorite Gospel artists was an internal transition from fan to servant. I stopped seeing artists as otherworldly people to simply admire and celebrate, and began to see them as real men and women with specific needs. Although I did not know it, that shift marked the beginning of my developing compassion for artists.

For me, developing compassion came through prayer for those individuals. Although I believe in the importance of an active prayer life, I cannot argue that everyone will learn compassion for artists primarily in that manner. For some of you, it may come through serving leaders in you local churches or by working in a charitable or volunteer capacity somewhere on an ongoing basis. The main point is to begin to learn to see the needs of others.

From outside the industry, it may not make sense that a person with all the advantages of celebrity would require compassion. The glare of the lights, the admiration of fans, the opportunities to travel, and the chance to make a living at something you love should be reason to celebrate. Most of the time, I'm sure it is.

But as soon as I stepped into the industry, I began to see the cost—the physical, emotional, and spiritual toll most artists pay in exchange for the chance to do what they love. I also began to see that often it is not the fans who place the greatest demand on artists. Many times it is those of us in the Business Community who require our artists to be at peak creative form while bearing the weight of productivity. We may greet them with passion, but frequently we fail to meet them with compassion.

At the top of our discussion of the Business Community, I said, "The needs and goals of big business can often be in conflict with the needs and goals of artistry." An unfortunate side effect of the intersection of art and commerce is an ongoing tension between the Creative Community and the Business Community. To put it more frankly, because money is at stake, it can be difficult for artists and industry workers to genuinely value and identify with each other's needs and concerns.

Although it may not be possible to eliminate that tension completely, I have learned that one key to overcoming it is to approach my artists, producers, and songwriters compassionately. Rather than going into each creative meeting or negotiation looking to maximize my own agenda, I have learned to listen to the needs of others and look for win-win scenarios.

It takes an experienced ear to hear the difference between a want and a true need; but having a heart for your creative partners goes a long way toward lifting the inherent tensions and moving toward effective alliances. The principle is simple: If I see you as my enemy, I will fight to the death. If, on the other hand, I choose to see you as my partner, I will look for ways to help you while acknowledging my own needs.

For those of us in the Business Community, I don't believe compassion for artists is optional. Quite frankly, we have no music industry jobs without the artists who produce our product.

Although you may be years away from a position of influence in the Gospel music industry, I believe it is vital to begin to consider these types of issues now. A repeated theme for me throughout our discussion is the fact that you cannot cram for the heart and character issues you will need in the moment you realize you need them.

The moment of crisis will never grant you the luxury to pause and prepare. Your preparation for success comes long before that moment. And because issues of your perspective, your character, and your heart are the most challenging to address, that work must begin now.

This brings us to our last of the three keys.

Key #3: A Willingness To Serve

Had I strategized and studied for my current career, I cannot tell you I would ever have recognized the need to trade my "fandom" for the posture of a servant. That concept was entirely contrary to the American ambition and idealism I embraced. I pursued higher education because I loved to learn, but certainly at the forefront of that pursuit was the desire to prepare myself for success—leadership, promotion, financial prosperity.

No one around me would have disagreed with my way of thinking. In fact, the people of greatest influence in my life—my parents and my Christian friends—supported my efforts in hopes of me gaining the titles and accolades they believed I deserved.

Throughout my educational career, I sought after every opportunity to gain experience and better prepare myself—internships, externships, freelancing for the school newspapers, student professional organizations. Simultaneously, I made great investments in my spiritual foundation, developing my prayer life and becoming active in campus ministry groups. Over time, I began to see that while the knowledge and experience I had were valuable tools, my perspective on how to use those tools needed an adjustment.

If you have read the book of Proverbs, you will see a repeating theme: **Humility always precedes promotion.**[20] Often in our society, we are led to believe the Bible was written by downtrodden people who developed their writings as a means of escape. We have this image of people abused by their circumstances, in need of an otherworldly faith to offset their everyday experiences.

That's why I find it so interesting that Solomon, the primary writer of Proverbs, was the wisest, wealthiest, and most celebrated man of his day. Leaders of other nations traveled far to hear his judgments and witness the riches of his kingdom. When a man of such great wealth and influence writes again and again of the connection between humility and promotion, we should listen!

It is a mistake to confuse humility or servanthood with the posture of being a doormat. In fact, in the early part of my process—in the final year before I was hired for my first industry job—I was surprised to find the opposite was true.

---

[20] Proverbs 15:33, Proverbs 18:12; Proverbs 22:4 *KJV*.

When I really began to let God pull me outside the comfort zone of my own ambition and take me into this foreign, new world of service, I began to gain real access to people of influence. Instead of waiting in the autograph line for the chance to hand an artist my business card, more and more I found myself being allowed backstage. Instead of asking for a phone number, I found those numbers being offered to me. And when my big break finally came, I could tell the person making the job offer felt they were actually gaining something in return.

The best part of all is that when those opportunities presented themselves, I was relieved of the desire to boast. Because my heart was in a new place, everything else followed. My goal shifted from what I could *get* to what I could *give*. My aim changed from short-term acquaintance with people of influence to long-term relationships. My attention was not on demonstrating how much I knew, but on learning from the experiences of others. Rather than to glory in my own accomplishment, I was grateful for a door I knew God had opened.

I believe that is true humility. True humility leads to promotion from the Lord, and that promotion should in turn make us more humble before Him.

I need you to know that I did **not** learn these lessons overnight. Although the initial shift in my career happened in a very concentrated period of time, the training was ongoing. There were many mistakes along the way, challenges from which I didn't expect to recover. In those moments, I learned more about God's grace and favor.

A word of caution: For those of you aspiring to the Business Community, these kinds of lessons are not popular. There are few places you will work where the heart of what we're discussing right now will be positively reinforced. But if you are intent on having a true and lasting impact in this marketplace and being of the greatest benefit to your creative partners, I would encourage you to embrace the words in this section most of all.

There will be moments when your corporate obligations will seem to require you to rely more on what you *know* than on who you *are*. That is the very reason we must become people of character. If you do the hard work of developing that character now, you will more wisely negotiate your way through those moments in the future.

Now, let's talk about more practical matters.

Roles Within The Business Community

At this point, you should be a bit more comfortable with the various parts of the Business Community and the general manner in which those parts interact. However, if you are serious about beginning a career on the industry side of Gospel music, it would be helpful to have a more detailed breakdown of each of those roles.

Even if you are relatively sure where your career is headed, I would encourage you to gain as much knowledge about the various roles as possible. As we will see shortly, the music marketplace is changing in drastic ways. Your continued success in this new world will depend on the diversity of your information along with the broadness of your experience.

Record Company Roles

Each record company has a unique business plan and structure, but they all tend to contain certain basic departments. Those departments reflect the manner in which the music industry has historically functioned over the past forty to fifty years. I'd like to offer you a brief overview of each role.

A&R

Historically, the term "A&R" stood for "Artists and Repertoire". An A&R representative typically scouted and discovered new talent and was also responsible for discovering and developing appropriate material for that talent to record and perform. Over the years, as record companies have shouldered less of the burden for the development of artists, the function of the A&R Department has morphed a bit toward "Artist Relations."

Nevertheless, of all of the departments within a record company, the A&R representatives work the most closely with artists, songwriters, and producers. They are the staff members responsible for facilitating the creative vision for a project, overseeing the budgets for those projects, and keeping them on schedule.

Important skills: A true ear for Gospel music, strong relationships with people throughout the Creative Community (especially artists, songwriters, producers, and their respective support teams—managers, engineers, publishers, etc.), a thorough understanding of the production process for CDs and DVD projects, knowledge of the legal aspects of production, the ability to create and maintain a budget, strong administrative and organizational skills.

Radio Promotions

Most of what we hear on the radio everyday is not random. In fact, often the songs on a radio station's playlist, along with the frequency with which those songs are played each day, are the result of the influence and hard work of radio promoters.

When an album is completed, it is the responsibility of the radio promotions staff to select the song(s) most likely to receive strong airplay. Although they may work in coordination with the artist and his management, it's their job to pick the hits.

It is also their responsibility to send that song to radio stations across the country and to exert their influence to maximize the amount of times that song is played. They do that through their relationships with programming directors and radio announcers, through promotional events and contests, and by basic radio tracking (polling of what stations are playing which songs, and how often).

Important skills: An ear for Gospel music, knowledge of the current Gospel radio marketplace, strong relationships with key members of the Gospel radio community (announcers, program directors, key members of the Gospel Announcers Guild, etc.), strong sales skills (including knowledge of product, the ability to talk/hype that product, persistence, and follow-through).

Publicity

A vital part of promoting a new CD or DVD is media coverage. Often the public will know that an artist has a new project on the horizon only when they read about it in their local newspaper, see a feature in their favorite magazine, or watch that artist perform his new music on their favorite talk show. Virtually without exception, all of those opportunities were created by a publicist.

The publicity department of a record company is responsible for creating and distributing press materials (press releases, bios, images, promotional copies of the product) to members of the media, including TV, print, and Internet outlets. Publicists also seek out major coverage opportunities for their artists and projects by pitching those artists and projects to the decision makers at those media outlets.

It is the publicist's job to secure interviews, reviews, features, and promotional appearances for the artist. They attempt to plug that artist into known media outlets, especially those likely to attract that artist's fans. The publicist's goal is to gain *unpaid* exposure for the artist.

Important skills: Strong written and oral communications skills, knowledge of the current media marketplace, relationships with key members of the media (writers, editors, TV producers), strong sales skills (including knowledge of product, the ability to talk/hype that product, persistence, and follow-through).

Marketing

The role of the marketing staff at a record label is quite broad. Typically, marketing people are responsible for positioning an artist and his CD in the marketplace through advertising, promotional activities, and events. Most of those efforts will involve *paid* exposure. In addition, a marketing director is normally responsible for the development of the visual elements of a CD, including the artwork and packaging, flyers, posters, postcards, etc.

Occasionally—depending on the structure of the record label—the marketing department may also be responsible for creating an Internet presence for the artists and projects. They do this by overseeing the content of label-owned web sites and by partnering with other web outlets to feature the artist and CD.

In addition, a marketing director is normally responsible for communicating the key information about each new CD to the members of the sales staff. They create the sales pages which will be circulated to retail outlets across the country to alert potential buyers to the content and vision of each new product.

Important skills: Creativity, knowledge of the current Gospel music marketplace, strong relationships with art directors, photographers, make-up artists, stylists, graphic designers, and web masters, event planning, and the ability to create and oversee large budgets.

Sales

The role of the sales staff is something about which you almost never hear until you actually work at a record label. Even after an artist is signed to a record deal, he may be introduced to key leaders within that label's sales department, but their roles are rarely explained very well.

The sales staff is responsible for developing a strong and consistent presence for the record label, its artists and products with key retailers and retail chains. They create and distribute the catalogues—containing sales pages on each new product—to retailers. More importantly, they work with buyers at key retail outlets to increase the number of copies of each product that will be bought by that retailer and to enhance the positioning and placement of those products in local stores.

Additionally, the sales staff is responsible for tracking the number of units sold on each CD or DVD and promoting re-orders of those items.

Important skills: Strong sales skills (including knowledge of product, the ability to talk/hype that product, persistence and follow-through), knowledge of the overall music retail landscape, strong relationships with buyers at key retailers.

Business Affairs (Legal)

For artists, the music industry may primarily be a creative environment, but for those of us on the industry side, the contract is king. From artist agreements to producer contracts, publishing licenses to sample clearances, there is almost no creative aspect of music that does not have a legal implication.

Consequently, all major labels have a legal department consisting of a staff of lawyers and their support personnel. It is their job to "paper" the specifics of the relationships between the label and all of its creative partners. The Business Affairs staff also advises the A&R and Marketing staff of content that could lead to legal challenges or potential law suits (libelous content).

Important skills: Accredited knowledge of entertainment law, strong relationships with key record label staff.

Hopefully you now have a more complete understanding of the record label environment from the industry perspective. It may seem like a vast amount of information, but record companies are only one part of the Business Community. With that in mind, let's move on.

Radio

For decades, radio stations have been the starting point for artists to launch their new albums. You might call radio the ground zero of the music promotion and marketing world. Even in the age of new media, file sharing, and music downloading, there is—at least for the moment—no quicker, more universal method of getting new music to the public ear.

The world of Gospel radio consists primarily of stations, radio announcers (the people who play the music and do the talk), and program directors (the people who decide what gets played and in what manner). Stations may be independently owned or part of a national chain of stations (network). Individual shows may even be syndicated—sold station-by-station for broadcast as part of the overall programming mix.

A key organization within the Gospel music world is the Gospel Announcers Guild (GAG), an auxiliary of the Gospel Music Workshop of America (GMWA). Founded in 1970, the group is a professional trade organization that addresses the needs and concerns of Gospel radio announcers and provides on-air personalities with an industry-wide presence.

Important skills: Strong oral communication skills, a love and ear for Gospel music, thorough knowledge of the broadcasting environment.

Media (TV, print, Internet)

Media is perhaps the most diverse sector of the Business Community. The media consists of various outlets through which we receive our information, including TV (news and entertainment shows), print (newspapers and magazines), and Internet (information, entertainment, and social web sites).

While there are many media outlets dedicated to Gospel music information, media coverage of Gospel artists, products, and issues appears freely throughout mainstream media as well.

Key members of the media are writers, editors, publishers, TV producers, and web masters.

Important skills: Strong written and oral communication skills, knowledge of the overall Gospel music industry, knowledge of broadcasting methods.

Managers

The artist manager is the individual who supervises, directs, and develops every aspect of a Gospel artist's career. In mainstream music, this individual is normally referred to as the personal manager, while the business manager handles the money, and the road manager is responsible for the artist during touring and travel. Generally speaking, in Gospel music the line between these roles is not quite as clearly drawn. In our marketplace, people tend to wear more hats.

Within the Business Community, the manager's job is the most comprehensive because he is the link between the artist and every other member of the Business, Creative, and Church Communities. Over the course of his job, a manager will interact on the artist's behalf with the record company and promoters. He will be a point person for the artist with radio and media. Additionally, the manager will often connect the artist to song-writers and producers and be the main contact for churches who book the artist to perform.

The manager is the coach of the artist's support team. He will often hire and supervise all the other members of an artist's team, including attorneys, booking agents, road managers, musicians, and—when necessary—independent publicists and independent radio promoters.

To do all of those things well, a manager must understand an artist's creative vision and then devise and execute a plan for that vision to develop and grow. He does this primarily by identifying and gathering the necessary tools to facilitate that artist's vision and then making sure those tools work well together. With those things in mind, a good manager's knowledge must be broad and his experiences diverse.

Important skills: Strong interpersonal skills, strong relationships with key people throughout the Gospel music industry, written and oral communication skills, knowledge of the music production process, management skills, the ability to nurture creative personalities, strong negotiation skills, basic knowledge of entertainment law, a comprehensive knowledge of the Gospel music industry.

Booking Agents

It is the job of a booking agent to secure paid performance engagements for the artist. The agent will be the point person for churches, organizations, and promoters seeking talent for their events. He will negotiate the terms of those agreements and often receive payments on the artist's behalf in connection with those events.

The booking agent will keep and organize the artist's appearance itinerary and circulate that itinerary to key members of the artist's team.

Important skills: Strong oral and written communication skills, good organizational skills, negotiation skills, relationships with key members of the Church Community, and promoters.

Promoters

Promoters are the people who plan, execute, and in some cases, sponsor live events where artists are showcased. In the Gospel music world, most often promoters are individuals or limited partnerships with strong ties to local churches.

The promoter secures the venue (facility where the event will be held), works with audio/visual companies to provide the sound and lighting, works with booking agents and managers to secure the artists, and then advertises, markets, and promotes the event for maximum success.

More experienced promoters may design and promote tours (a series of concerts featuring the same roster of artists in a variety of cities). The main goals are to attract a significant audience, showcase key artists, and show a profit.

Important skills: Event planning and coordination, relationships with key churches, booking agents and managers, strong sales and marketing skills.

Retail

As we will see, retail is the area in which the most drastic changes are occurring at this moment in the music industry. The main reason is the impact of new media on the music-buying habits of consumers. Because people acquire and utilize music much differently today than they did twenty—or even ten—years ago, the nature and functionality of retail outlets has changed dramatically.

A retailer can be a physical store where you purchase music (also known as brick-and-mortar retailers), or a variety of Internet sales outlets, including web versions of brick-and-mortar stores (eg. Target.com, WalMart.com), on-line exclusive outlets (eg. Amazon.com) or digital outlets such as iTunes, Rhapsody, or Snocap.

Because of the changes in the retail world, there has probably never been a time of greater opportunity for retailers with an Internet business plan. At the same time, there has never been a more difficult time for the independent brick-and-mortar outlets with music as their primary product. More about that a bit later.

Important skills: Sales knowledge and experience, a working knowledge of the overall music landscape (especially artists and record companies), business administration skills

Now that we've taken a closer look at the basic roles in the Business Community, how exactly do you begin?

First Steps

The Business Community is quite diverse. As a result, there are a variety of different paths for an aspiring industry executive. The person aiming to become an artist manager would have a very different career path than the individual who wants to work in radio or retail. An individual hoping to finish as a successful promoter would need very different work experience and specialized knowledge than the aspiring publicist. The thing they will all share, however, is the Gospel music marketplace.

Many pages ago, we looked at the manner in which the parts of the Business Community have historically overlapped (see pages 20–21). The various functions within the Business Community are so interconnected that the retailer and concert promoter do not have the luxury to ignore radio. Likewise, record companies cannot isolate themselves from managers and booking agents. And certainly all of us will have to work with artists.

With those things in mind, I firmly believe the person who will make the most of his career in Gospel music is the one who *studies the overall Gospel music marketplace.* The more you develop a context for this industry, the more you will be able to maximize your experiences.

Rather than simply turning to the classified section of a music industry trade magazine and mailing your résumé to every company with a "help wanted" entry, I would encourage you to consider the long term. What are your long-range goals for yourself?

Don't just consider your current qualifications. What skills would you like to gain? What experiences would enhance what you already know? Those should be guiding questions as you *prayerfully* begin to plot a course for yourself.

Most people with a college education or comparable work experience could gain an entry level music industry position. However, becoming a true person of influence will require quite a bit more. For those of you who would aspire to have an *impact* on the industry side of Gospel music, I would like to offer the following pieces of practical advice.

Advice: Attend Industry Conferences And Conventions.

In the spring of 1992, about six months before I started my first job in Gospel music, I had the opportunity to speak with a well-known Gospel artist about my aspirations. One of the key pieces of advice he gave me was to begin attending industry conferences and conventions.

When he gave me that recommendation, I must admit I was a little disappointed. I was only a few months from graduation, and my primary hope was for that conversation to end in a job offer. Things didn't turn out that way, but I took his advice to heart.

A few months later, I had the opportunity to go to a huge music industry event sponsored by a well-known Christian music company. It required me to pay my own airfare, hotel, and food for a week. At the time, it was a considerable financial investment for me because I had graduated a few months earlier without a job. Nevertheless, I believed the opportunity was from the Lord. I watched as He provided for my needs.

This would be a really cool story if I told you I went to the conference and was hired by a top company who just happened to send a human resources rep to the event looking for someone exactly like me. That didn't happen.

What did happen that week was this: The work I had been doing, trying to hear from the Lord and to understand just what He was calling me to do began to pay off. At every event I attended, as I watched and listened and asked questions, I received information that confirmed my call to this market-place. I also received tons of encouraging words from the most unlikely sources.

Each day nudged me a bit closer toward clarity, and by the end of the week, I was sure I was hearing from God. Although I still had no clue about where or when my first job would come, I was committed to continuing to study this marketplace and serving wherever I could until a door opened.

The seminars they offered at the conference, along with the clinicians and other attendees I met, helped me broaden my sense of the industry. The information I learned there helped me understand a bit more about my strengths, while preparing me for challenges I was likely to face.

When I returned home, I had the most unexpected happy ending. My answering machine was full of messages from the artist I had spoken to six months earlier.

I returned the call, apologizing that I had been out of town at an industry conference. The fact that I had taken his advice seriously and invested in myself left an impression. He offered me my first job in the industry.

Now I can't promise you a trip to an industry conference will result in a job. I can promise you that your commitment to invest in yourself will impress future bosses. It's part of being a "go-getter." People who show the desire to take the initiative, will always rise to the top of the résumé heap. And even if you don't get that first job right away, you will be more informed and more connected when you finally do.

I would encourage you to embrace your early conference experiences. Even if you don't walk away with the business card of the person who will become your first boss, you should walk away with a broader, more accurate concept of the industry.

Never forget this: As a consumer, your knowledge of the Gospel music industry will only get you so far. Once you've decided to make the transition from consumer to aspiring industry person, your success will in large part be determined by the accuracy of your concept of the Gospel music marketplace.

If you focus on *learning* (attending sessions, reading the available materials, etc.) and *listening* and not simply on *networking*, conferences can truly help you refine your concept of the marketplace. They are often the first chance you will have to apply and test your Gospel music knowledge in the real world.

I have attended many such industry conferences in connection with my work. Unfortunately, the majority of the aspiring industry people I have met at those events were more eager to show how much they already knew than to take the opportunity to listen to people who are currently making a career in the marketplace. Somehow they were convinced that if they threw out the right names or associated themselves—however distantly—with the right artists, they would be embraced as peers.

If you forget everything else we've discussed here, please remember this: **Hype will never be a suitable substitute for substance.** Those who talk, learn to produce hype. Those who listen and watch tend to develop substance.

A good place to begin might be with two of the longest running Gospel music conferences:

1) The Gospel Music Association's (GMA) Annual Music Week, *www.gospelmusic.org*
2) The Gospel Music Workshop Of America's (GMWA) Annual Convention, *www.gmwanational.org*

Gospel music conferences can be costly. So get the most out of your financial investment. Choose your conferences wisely and go with an eagerness to learn and connect. Watch, listen, and grow. Opportunities are likely to follow.

Advice: Subscribe To An Industry Trade Magazine.

One of the best ways to learn about the overall music industry is subscribing to *and actually reading* a music industry trade magazine. By "trade magazine" I mean a publication that specifically targets an industry *from the perspective of those who work in that industry*. Unlike general interest magazines—even those with a music focus—a trade publication will help you gain insight and information about your chosen field from the insider's perspective.

The publication I have found to be the most helpful is *Billboard* magazine. *Billboard*, a weekly magazine, is known as "the world's premier music publication" and has been covering entertainment and music industry issues since 1894. Because it is written *by* music industry insiders, primarily *for* music industry insiders, the features and news stories provide key information regarding every aspect of the music industry—new releases, company launches and mergers, airplay and sales charts, classifieds (including job postings), legal developments, etc.

As an added feature, *Billboard* structures its sections by musical genre. You can focus on whatever types of music are most relevant to you. Their coverage of Gospel music is generally broad and insightful.

Billboard is a comprehensive trade magazine; therefore, the cost of a subscription is considerably higher than a standard newsstand publication (approximately $300 per year vs. $25–$50 per year for your average magazine). The language is also geared toward true industry people. With that in mind, it may take you several issues to begin to get a feel for what's happening. Be encouraged. The time and money you spend will be worthwhile investments.

This may not seem like an important first step, but it truly is. Even though you might not understand everything you're reading, don't give up. Over time, you will begin to gain not just understanding, but insight as well.

I've found that a key difference between people who simply have jobs and people whose journeys leave large footprints in their respective marketplaces is the ability to understand the long-term, broad impact of their choices and efforts.

I don't believe it's enough to simply learn your job well enough to get by. To become a person of true influence, it is necessary to be able to apply factual knowledge within a broader context. In fact, that is my preferred definition of wisdom—the application of knowledge.

Much like the difference between a newspaper and a news-magazine, a good trade magazine doesn't simply relate facts. It adds perspective to those facts, making it possible for us to see trends and understand the reasons behind them. When you mix those forms of knowledge with significant work experiences, it becomes much easier to anticipate change.

I believe most marketplace leaders will tell you that a big key to their success is the ability to remain one step ahead of the crowd. Their ability to anticipate change gives them the advantage of being able to build a plan in advance rather than being forced to simply learn to survive after the change has happened.

The preparation for that level of leadership begins now. Make the investment in your industry knowledge and look for work experiences where you can humbly apply it.

Advice: Do An Internship With An Artist Management Company.

I'm sure the first instinct for anyone hoping to land a job on the industry side of Gospel music is to secure an internship at a record company. In fact, it is not a requirement of most entry level record company jobs for your résumé to show an internship at a label. It will certainly help you to have a broader understanding of the record company world, but I've known lots of people—present company included—who landed record company jobs without that particular experience.

Don't get me wrong, completing an internship with a record label may be a good idea. However, I'd like to make a suggestion that will give you a unique edge.

We've already talked about the basic tension between the Creative and Business Communities. I am convinced that a key factor in that tension is the simple reality that artists and industry people do not spend enough time living within each other's worlds.

We've all heard the saying that you should never judge a man until you've walked a mile in his shoes. In other words, the ability to understand and empathize with a person is the key to righteous judgment. With that in mind, I've always believed that many of the tensions between industry workers and artists could be resolved if more industry workers were required to complete an internship with an artist management company or within an artist's team (or "camp").[21]

It may seem strange, but there are certain "cultural" differences between artists and industry people. Artists tend to value art over commerce, the vision over the timeline, and concept over process. Core values for industry people tend to fall on the opposite ends of those pairs. Corporate commitments require commerce, timeline, and process to be prioritized. It would seem impossible to reconcile the two sides. Many days it certainly feels that way.

One of the greatest gifts the Lord provided in my work history was to give me my first industry job *not* at a record company, but at a management and production company owned and operated by an artist. Living on that side of the industry for so many years gave me an understanding of the needs and perspectives of an artist in a way I didn't truly value until I spent my first year working at a record company.

---

[21] Depending on the structure an artist has established, an artist's camp might include administrative or personal assistants, musicians and singers, and members of the artist's road crew (including road manager, merchandise manager, and sound tech).

It would be impossible for me to outline every lesson I learned from that experience, but two particularly valuable bits of insight I gained during those years are: (1) the real world impact of music sales, and (2) the value the artist places on his music.

The Real World Impact Of Music Sales.

During my college years, I purchased more than my share of cassettes and CDs. If I heard that a new project from one of my favorite artists was on the way, I made sure to get to the music store within the first week of sales. And when I found a new Gospel album that I was excited about, I would sometimes drive my friends to the store with me, so we could all buy our own copies.

Despite my purchasing habits, I don't think it ever occurred to me that my decision to buy a CD actually impacted the livelihood of those artists. I'm not sure where I thought their money was coming from, but I never considered that my decision to buy, rather than to copy or borrow, their new projects had any real-world impact.

All of that changed for me when I began working directly with an artist.

Up-close and personal, I saw how our paychecks were impacted by the abundance or lack of CD sales at retail outlets and at our merchandise table after our shows.

It became harder to remain a silent bystander when people would stand in front of the CD shelf or in front of our "merch" table and barter between each other over who would buy which CD and let the other person burn it. I knew their decision had a direct effect on how I was likely to live and eat over the next month.

That experience impacted me as a consumer, but more importantly, it impacted me as an industry professional. Some years later when I was working at a record label, I saw how easy it was to consider music sales only in terms of things like chart position and market share, or to quickly celebrate or dismiss an album based upon the first week numbers.

Life in the corporate world often offers the comfort of a regular paycheck, regardless of the sales from one CD release. Honestly that's one of the great benefits of working on the industry side of music. But if that world is the only one to which you've been exposed in this industry, I'm afraid your perspective will be severely limited.

For me, the opportunity to feel the impact on my personal wallet of successful or unsuccessful album sales shaped me as an industry person. It kept me from developing an "oh well" mentality after a disappointing street week.[22] It made me aware of the story behind the numbers. Most importantly, I believe it kept me focused on the importance of my everyday efforts as a contributing factor to the success—or failure—of my projects. In other words, it made me work harder.

The Value The Artist Places On His Music.

I honestly believe those of us who work in Gospel music have the privilege of representing some of the finest musicians, singers, and songwriters in the world.

While we may recognize the passion in the music or the impact a particular hit song may have on consumers, it can be difficult to understand the personal importance those songs have to the

---

[22] The first week of retail sales for a CD or DVD is called "street week." It is the week when the project first becomes available to consumers, or first hits the street. It is considered a strong predictor of the overall sales impact of an album, and unfortunately, many times a measure of the commercial value of an artist's career at that moment.

artists who recorded them—particularly if those artists were also the songwriters and/or producers of that material.

I once had the opportunity to sit in the room while one of my artists was being interviewed by a member of the press. The writer asked the artist which one of the songs on her current album was her favorite. To that, the artist cheerfully, but intently replied, "Wow. I'm not sure I can answer that question. It would be like telling you which one of my children I love the most."

It was a simple statement and one I've heard other artists echo over the years. It is a valuable sentiment to keep in mind in our daily work in this marketplace. Unfortunately, that sentiment can quickly become dulled or lost as we, in our roles as industry executives, turn our attention primarily toward issues of commerce.

One of the most valuable experiences during my first job in Gospel music was the opportunity to watch as albums began to take shape, individual songs moving from passing ideas to fully produced tracks and unrelated tunes coming together to form an album. The moment when the finishing touches are placed on the final mix and a collection of songs begins to feel like an album continues to be a powerful moment for me.

For artists who remain thoroughly involved in the production of their albums, in many ways the completion of a project is akin to the birthing process. It is deeply personal and full of dreams. An album is often an expression of the artist's emotional experiences and realizations at that moment in his life. And for the Gospel artist, it is frequently connected to his relationship with and revelations about God.

So when the artist delivers an album to his record company, it is an extremely sensitive moment. If that artist has stretched creatively or shown new sides of himself on a particular project, there may be elements of fear for that artist. How the A&R person or closest member of the label staff reacts to that music—the manner in which we listen, understand, celebrate, or question that material—often feels to the artist as an acceptance or rejection of that artist *personally.*

Now I know it may be hard to believe that when you have only seen that artist on a stage singing their hearts out openly and confidently, even joyfully, before hundreds or thousands of people. But there is a huge difference between the artist's relationship to the fans and his relationship to the industry.

Fans are there because they already believe in the artist's vision and place value on the artist's music. The proof of that is the fact that they have purchased a ticket and taken a few hours out of their busy lives to sit and listen.

But to the artist, we in the industry are the skeptical gatekeepers. We are the ones who will decide what the public hears and when. We are the ones whose support, or lack thereof, will often determine if the artist will continue to have a chance to be heard and embraced. Our love is the first one. And when it's not there, even if that artist chooses to march on in confidence, I'm afraid damage is done.

In my roles as a radio promoter, A&R person, and manager, I've witnessed that **moment of first risk**—when the artist plays new music for the first time or sings me an idea for a song—over and over again. No matter where the artist is in his career cycle, I've seen that same flicker of hesitation or expectation, as they wait for my reaction.

I honestly believe seeing that process behind-the-scenes—as an insider to the artist's camp—so early in my career helped me take that moment seriously. And in much the same way that I had to learn how to hold another person's newborn child for the first time—I had to learn how to support my artists through the moment of first risk.

It is a lesson I have not allowed myself to forget over the years, even as corporate demands made it less and less popular for me to care.

Again, I know of few places in this marketplace where you will be encouraged to embrace the sentiments of artistry. But if we are to rise above the role of salesmen and aspire to the calling of service in this industry, I believe we have to strike a balance.

For me, the first step in finding that balance has always been to understand the heart and vision of my artist. Only when I know that can I rightly identify the best way to accomplish that vision, the audience for the project and the correct method for connecting the project to that audience. Looked at in that light, the choice to embrace the artist's heart is just good business.

Before we move on, I want to be clear about this: I am *not* talking about becoming a "yes" person. To simply agree with everything your artist says or creates will not gain that artist's trust, nor help you build authentic relationships with your creative partners.

However, if you value the artistic weight of the projects and if you are successful at expressing your appreciation for the artist's process, you will be able to influence and effect change in ways that help the artist communicate his vision in a commercially viable manner.

I think it's important to note that I had the advantage of working for an artist who was also a producer. Because the majority of our work was *not* on albums featuring my boss, my industry experience became rather broad. We had the chance to interact with a variety of record labels, industry staff, artists, and management companies. Consequently, by comparing my experiences with those outside systems, I was able to learn what things were indeed essential and fundamental elements of the business practices in this marketplace.

When I accepted my first position at a record label, certainly my perspective changed. My new corporate obligations required me to learn and enact a different set of values, but I never lost a keen awareness of the needs and perspectives of the artists on our roster.

That awareness enabled me to do my job well and still maintain positive relationships with my artists—on good days as well as in crisis. My empathy enabled me to establish a real trust with my artists that actually helped me meet most of my corporate obligations, while still honoring the majority of my artists' needs.

I've had the distinct pleasure to work with many different, highly qualified music industry executives. I learned so much from all of them. But one of the most interesting things to me was that those executives who had the benefit of working closely with or around artists in the earliest years of their careers seemed to have more positive relationships with artists *throughout* their careers. Since ultimately so much of our work is dependent upon the trust and creativity of our artists, positive relationships enabled those executives to accomplish the goals of the company while maintaining artist satisfaction.

I cannot stress this enough: For those of us who make our careers on the industry side of Gospel music, the artist is not our enemy. Without them, we have no product. To work well with them is a matter of our corporate survival. However, in my opinion, mere corporate survival is not enough. I would much rather excel at my job while simultaneously building trust with my creative partners.

The best way I know to lay a foundation for that mindset is to begin your career by walking a mile in an artist's shoes. Do yourself a long-range favor. Look for your first internship opportunity on the creative side of the industry.

The Value Of Excellence

The greatest encouragement I can give to anyone who is seeking a career in the Business Community is this: **Always pursue excellence.** For those of us blessed to steward the music of the Gospel—regardless of the sector of the industry to which we are called—excellence must be our foundation, our overriding method, and an essential part of our end goal.

It may seem to be a rather obvious piece of advice. Why wouldn't anyone want to give their very best at all times? I believe that most people do indeed want to become good at what they do. The problem is that we are often misinformed about *how* to become truly good at what we do.

Taking cues from what we see in the media, our society as a whole has been trained to value spin over facts and hype over truth. On a daily basis, a great deal of what we learn about the world around us is delivered with an eye toward sensationalism rather than information or education. Hype is indeed the rule of the day, with the most-often-repeated misperceptions actually replacing the truth in the minds of most Americans.

As music industry professionals, we use that concept to our advantage. Much of our work is based upon attempts to capture the attention of the music buyer in a highly competitive marketplace.

Therefore, our ability to stress the merits of our product the most loudly, the most consistently, and the most convincingly will often determine the degree of our success. To put it more plainly, hype is a primary methodology for selling CDs.

For those of us on the industry side of music, that reality brings with it a great dilemma: What works the best for us in our interaction with the consumer can become a great liability to us professionally.

Throughout the music industry—on both the creative and business sides—there is an unfortunate tendency to hype our affiliations or connections rather than focus on investing in and developing our own skill set. How many times have you heard the phrase, "It's not *what* you know, but *who* you know that counts?" That's what I like to call **entourage disease**: The belief that you are great by virtue of your associations rather than by reason of your personal skills or accomplishments.

I know we tend to think of this primarily as a mindset on the creative side of the industry. From singers and background vocalists to songwriters, musicians, and producers, the creative field is extraordinarily competitive. Even among truly talented individuals, the difference between breaking through and fading away can often be a matter of which key person you meet at what key moment. It may appear that timing is everything, but I promise you when it comes to *lasting* success, preparation means a lot more.

Surprisingly, the same concepts apply to the industry side of music. This is a highly competitive field with a limited number of job opportunities. Key positions in the Gospel music marketplace are certainly even more limited than those within mainstream music.

Against that backdrop, it is understandable that an aspiring industry executive might spend time hyping his associations ("name-dropping") or overselling his skills in an attempt to land a position. It is easy to see why a person might fill his résumé with high-profile projects when, in reality, he may hold only very loose associations to those projects. In the era of hype, we are led to believe those tactics work.

A person who chooses to grasp success in such a manner may land a job or two. He may even manage to glide along with *apparent* success. But all the hype in the world will not teach you what to do when you have a real project on the line and a corporate system looking to you for results. All the name-dropping you can muster will not replace actual relationships with key songwriters, producers, and artists when you've got to call-in favors to meet a deadline.

I've learned it is more valuable to make a personal commitment to developing your skill set consistently over time than to settle for *appearing* successful publicly. It is far better to spend your time becoming excellent.

Let's not confuse the commitment to excellence with being a perfectionist. None of us will ever be flawless, and our attempts to develop beyond the possibility of error will meet with ongoing disappointment.

The commitment to excellence to which I am referring has the following statement at its heart:

> *Whatever you do, work at it with all your heart, as working for the Lord, not for men, since you know that you will receive an inheritance from the Lord as a reward. It is the Lord Christ you are serving.* (Colossians 3:23–24, NIV)

When the Apostle Paul made this statement, he was not addressing people in ministry. On the contrary, he was speaking to Christians who found it their lot to be either slaves or servants. He was giving people, who were required to labor under less than ideal conditions, tools to apply their faith to their everyday circumstances.

In our careers in the music industry, we will certainly enjoy more freedoms and benefits than Paul's audience. Nevertheless, the principle remains the same. Wherever we are called to work—even in the commercial world of recorded music—we are to have the perspective and posture of servants of God. We may be employed by large corporations or family-run businesses, and some of us may even have the fortune to become entrepreneurs. Regardless of the environment, our ultimate boss is the Lord.

Paul's words do not give us the license to disregard or disrespect our immediate bosses. On the contrary, they provide us with the basis for an abiding conviction. Our faith should inform and shape our working lives.

As a person of faith, I should aspire to give the greatest service, to possess the strongest work ethic, and to achieve the most consistent results. As a person of faith in the working world, it is my duty to develop the commitment to excellence. Even though I am working for people, the focus of my efforts should always be God's approval. Every day He deserves my very best.

With that in mind, here are a few key ideas that I hope will aid you in this pursuit.

Give Careful Attention To The Basics.
Anyone who has ever played competitive sports for any length of time can tell you that the best coaches always kill their players with the **fundamentals**. Ugh, the fundamentals!

When I was in junior high school, my gym teacher spent one year focusing on various sports as a series of "units." Within that year, we studied a variety of sports—basketball, field hockey, softball, even archery—each for a limited number of weeks. During each unit, we had the opportunity to play the sport; but for several sessions before that, we were required to endure actual note-taking lessons on the history of that sport, the basic rules, and the core skills involved.

When we arrived at the unit on basketball, I remember thinking how odd it was for us to be sitting taking notes on basics like where and when basketball was invented[23] when several of my classmates were already competing in the sport after school in intramural games. In fact, it was in one such intramural game that I learned an embarrassing life lesson.

There I was taking the ball downcourt, surrounded by the sound of far too many oversized, preteen-girl feet squeaking across the gymnasium floor. In a show of support, many of the junior high boys had come to watch this relatively unimportant game.

For me it was a rare public moment. Quite shy in non-academic settings, I was not prepared for the rush of coming off the break after an opponent had scored, and leading my team toward our basket at the other end of the court. I remember feeling the energy and, with no experiential point of reference, beginning to channel what I had seen on sports highlight reels and in basketball movies. I slowed down, listened to the sounds, looked into the stands, smiled and milked the moment.

And then it happened…

---

[23] Springfield, MA in 1891 by James Naismith.

Out of the blue, the same girl who had scored for the opposing team only seconds earlier flew by me. All I saw was a streak of brown wearing a headband and a ponytail and then she was gone. Before I could mentally register the motion, she had stolen the ball from me and was back to her team's basket for another score. The junior high boys went crazy in the stands! I remained frozen at midcourt. I don't remember ever playing basketball competitively again.

Don't feel bad for me. In my mind, this is an embarrassing moment, but funny nevertheless. Fortunately for me, God didn't call me to play basketball!

The lesson for me was this: While I was busy relishing the glitter of the moment, someone who had for years made it her ongoing and consistent goal to master the fundamentals had simply bested me. Rather than relish her first score or to become distracted by the people in the stands, she kept her eye on my moves and on the ball. When an opportunity presented itself to score a second time, she simply applied the basic skills she had been fine-tuning in private.

I knew that player well and even had the chance to be her teammate in varsity volleyball a few years later. She took sports seriously and had come to that game the same way she came to every game—prepared. Her basic basketball skills served her well, enabling her to take advantage of my lack of discipline. And in the moment, in that most important moment when others were watching, she scored on me big time.

I wanted to be seen. My opponent wanted to win.

At the risk of overloading you with sports references, legendary football coach Paul "Bear" Bryant said, "It's not the will to win, but the will to *prepare* to win that makes the difference." I believe that is the secret to pursuing excellence. Preparation requires us to take our minds off the dream of public triumph and to instead focus on the most basic, uncelebrated, often monotonous details. Excellence will always begin with those small, unseen things.

Depending on which road you are planning to take in the Business Community, the required skills may be quite different. However, I have found three basics that apply to all of us industry folk. They are:

- Attention to detail
- Good oral & written communication skills
- Clear, consistent follow-up

Those most basic of skills are the cornerstone to any successful career in business. Not only will those three things help you get your foot in the door initially, they will help you earn the attention of your bosses and the respect of your peers. Those are the skills that make you a reliable go-to person for bigger responsibilities. And when you are really good at those basics, there will be an added, secret bonus. Please lean into the page as I whisper this one:

At the start of a new job when you are still lacking in the specialized skills and experience you will need to thrive in that position, *those three basics will buy you time while you learn.*

I discovered the weight of that truth in the early weeks of my first record label job. The company to which I was hired was a brand new division in a family of well-established record labels. Wisely, they chose to grow slowly, with a limited number of artists and a minimally-sized staff. Consequently, I was hired for the hybrid position of Manager, Radio Promotion & Media Relations.

In that role, it was my responsibility to create and execute the national radio plans for all of our CD releases, while simultaneously creating and executing the national publicity plans for those same releases. In addition, because our label was new, it was a large part of my job to forge a general media and radio presence for our company among the established stations (including key announcers and organizations) and media outlets (local, regional, and national TV, print, and Internet).

Did I mention this was my *very first* record label position?

Although at that point I had worked for more than six years in the Gospel music industry, I definitely did *not* walk into the door adequately prepared to ace so many key responsibilities. But I knew I was called to be at that company. I believed God had given me something valuable for those artists. More importantly, I knew He had called me there to grow.

I had to make the decision to learn as much as I could, as well as I could, and as quickly as possible. In the meantime, I focused on my strengths—the three basics.

On "day one," I didn't know very much about picking a radio hit, and I was only vaguely familiar with the overall Gospel radio landscape. However, I was good at speaking on the phone and in person. I knew how to write effective letters and emails, and I was excellent at follow-up.

I quickly began to apply those skills. I disciplined myself to follow-up on all of my first-time encounters with radio announcers, program directors, station managers, and members of the Gospel Announcers Guild. Whenever I received a new business card, I followed up. Whenever I received a request for product, it was in the mail as quickly as possible with a note and my contact information. That was the rule each time and every time. No exceptions.

I watched and listened to the needs of my new radio and media partners and used the basics to meet those needs wherever possible. I worked hard to make up for what I didn't yet know with the skills that I already possessed.

Another important example of that concept came in the execution of my publicity duties. Initially, I lacked key relationships at major TV media. I wasn't able to get my artists on TV right away, but I was able to gain exposure for them and my company in local and regional print media simply by focusing on the basics.

I quickly learned that many local and regional newspapers did not have full-time entertainment and event writers. Using my written communication skills, I was able to capitalize on that knowledge by providing press materials with high enough quality to run "as is." Since those editors didn't need to spend time on changes and the pieces were complete enough not to require a writer to follow-up, they ran with what I gave them.

Within a relatively short period of time, I began to see that my artists benefited from my efforts. Their press releases, bios, and photos ran regularly in those print publications, giving them a presence in markets where they were not yet known.

While I worked to learn the skills and build the relationships I didn't have at the beginning, my attention to the basics paid off. My bosses were pleased, and my artists could hear themselves on the radio and see themselves in publications where they had never appeared before.

Most importantly, I began to build lasting relationships with key people at radio and in the media, which enabled me to do my job more effectively. Focusing on the basics bought me the time to develop those things. I was able to be effective rather than to stress over what I didn't yet know.

Perhaps it would have been more ambitious to try to impress my bosses right away with the promise of a major TV appearance or by proposing an aggressive plan to get a single added to one of the key urban stations. I can't say those things would have been wrong, but I do know they were not likely to have been successful at that stage in our company's history and at that time in my professional development. I am certain that kind of hype would have caused me to miss important opportunities for building a presence for our company and our artists.

One of the hardest things in the world is to maintain focus on the essential things when you work in a hype-oriented industry. It can be quite difficult to do the tedious work of learning and honing the details of your craft, particularly when your peers in the industry may be celebrated and promoted ahead of you.

Rest assured that time spent honing the fundamentals is never a waste. The basic skills you make the time to perfect now will always be yours to build upon. The basics are the means by which you will become a person of substance. And as I've said many times by now, substance ultimately wins over hype—always.

Don't Be Distracted By Titles.

It may seem strange, but one of the greatest hindrances to excellence is the pursuit of titles. "Sr. Director of this" and "VP of that" have a powerful sound. As a motivating source, however, they can become a roadblock by causing you to concentrate on the wrong things.

As professionals in this industry, our will to succeed should not be rooted in outward signs of our achievement. Instead, our aspirations should be founded upon the desire to be of greatest service along with the commitment to have the most positive influence. Focusing on outward achievements can lead us toward self-promotion and superficiality. Maintaining a heart for service and positive influence, on the other hand, challenges us to listen, learn, and develop real skills.

When I first began reading *Billboard* magazine, one of my favorite columns was Executive Turntable. In that section, they announced new appointments and promotions and included photos of key industry people.

One week about four years into my first industry job, I was reading that column when I came across a blurb about one of my college classmates whom I had not seen in a long time. Throughout our school years, he had dreamed of pursuing a career in music, so it was exciting to see that things were going so well for him.

I reached out to congratulate him, and he began to recount for me some of the wonderful experiences and opportunities he'd had. He had just bought a house and was purchasing a new car, and he was excited about attending an exclusive event in his area that week. I was glad to have had the opportunity to reconnect.

In the coming days, a little, gray cloud slowly began hanging over my thoughts. I found myself comparing my life to my friend's life. I didn't like what I saw. He had gone into his first music industry job immediately out of college, while I had gone on to journalism school. As I was still learning to hear the voice of God regarding the Gospel music industry, my friend was already working on major projects and making valuable connections.

At that moment in my life, although I was sure I had been obedient to the Lord, I had very little *outward* evidence of success. I was making just enough to pay my bills and certainly couldn't afford to consider luxuries. I was sowing into a ministry I loved, and working with people who were like family to me, but I felt so far behind in my aspirations for myself and in the expectations of my family.

It is not that I begrudged my friend his success. I was genuinely happy for him and proud to have known him during his years of dreaming. Nevertheless, when I looked at the names and faces in that *Billboard* column, I saw what could have been. I saw titles I longed to have and jobs I should have been experienced enough to earn. Internally, I began to wrestle with my choices and struggle to understand God's plan for me.

I'd like to tell you that challenge resolved itself after only a few days. In a relatively short period of time, the Holy Spirit *did* help me to refocus and recommit to where I was, but that feeling of having lost time lingered at the back of my mind for quite a while. It's hard to give your all with joy when you are haunted by where you'd like to be.

Several years later, when I was working in my first record label position, I began to see things quite differently. Within weeks of being at a major record company, it became apparent just how quickly things shift in this business. In a very short period of time, positions can be earned or lost, companies can change hands or fold, deals can be announced with great fanfare and just as quickly dissolve.

In fact, so many changes and major announcements were made in my first few weeks at my new company that I pulled my boss to the side one day and asked if this was normal. He calmly reassured me. I went back to work.

In such a shifting environment, I quickly began to value God's process for me—the length of time I had spent learning to hear from God, the decision to take a position based upon a call to serve rather than the opportunity for advancement. So much of the internal, private work I'd had to do in the early years of my career gave me the character to remain centered and unwavering in my work ethic when I finally did earn my first title.

I became grateful for the years spent under the radar. That time enabled me to watch and listen and grow both spiritual and professional roots in a way I don't think I could have if my promotions had come sooner. If I had pushed ahead toward the titles that drew me rather than staying where the Lord had placed me, I might have gotten closer to my personal ambitions faster, but I don't believe I would have arrived with as much experience or such a broad set of skills.

In the years following, when new titles seemed to come quickly, I didn't allow my focus to change from the basics. I worked hard not to lose my passion for excellence. I truly believe those things kept me grounded under difficult and stressful circumstances.

Ultimately a person's title may be evidence of his opportunities, but it will never be a true mark of the level of his effectiveness. To ensure you arrive at your destiny with all the tools to succeed, it's important to maintain focus on these things: (1) mastering the skills you already have and (2) developing the ones you don't. Do those things well and titles are sure to follow.

Excellence Is Never Comparative.

One of the biggest errors we can make as professionals is to measure our own performance based upon the performance of others. I'm sure that statement seems odd when a large part of this industry is built upon comparisons like chart rankings, sales figures, and awards. In fact, it is *because* so much of our business involves those comparative systems that we must be so careful.

I once heard an executive comment on the fleeting nature of top-label status in this business. He pointed out two major companies that had been marketplace leaders in the 1970s and 1980s, massive brands that completely dominated the Gospel industry in their seasons. At the time of that conversation, both labels were entirely out of business, their catalogues[24] in jeopardy.

How does something like that happen? Truly the number one spot is fleeting by nature. The artist, CD, or company holding that top ranking becomes the target of every other competitor. People love to knock off the number one anything!

Nevertheless, there is a big difference between being knocked off the top rung and going out of business entirely. How in the world does something like that happen?

Obviously there are multiple factors involved. However, I believe one of the most significant causes is the pitfall of comparative excellence. Often, once we've become number one, because we have surpassed our competition, we lose the ability to remain critical of our own strengths and weaknesses.

We've all heard the saying, "If it ain't broke, don't fix it." The implication is that if something seems to be working, there is no need to question it. In reality, by the time most things have failed, many opportunities to recognize and address the problem have long passed. That is why success—especially top-level success in a competitive field like ours—can be so dangerous.

We need to begin with a different paradigm. Rather than competition, true excellence is the key.

Excellence never looks ahead to number one, never looks to the side to measure its progress and never looks over its shoulder to see who is gaining ground. Instead of being influenced by the outside world, true excellence requires us to look in two entirely

---

[24] The collection of recordings (masters) owned by a label is called their catalogue. These are the primary assets of any record label.

"other" directions. First, it requires us to look up to God—the ulti-mate standard bearer. Second, it requires us to look inward in an honest evaluation of our skills, our execution, and our motivations.

It is critical to realize that if God created me with a specific purpose and destiny, only He can set the guidelines for the man-ner in which I should achieve. His thoughts toward me should remain my primary influence. His plans for me should set the pace for my professional life.

My greatest inspiration for this concept is a moment in the life of Jesus. As always, He was being challenged by the Pharisees for the manner in which He conducted himself in ministry. His works, though admittedly good, fell outside of the boundaries of the literal law. So they questioned His intentions.

Look at His response:

> Jesus said to them, "My Father is always at his work to this very day, and I, too, am working.... I tell you the truth, the Son can do nothing by himself; he can do only what he sees his Father doing, because whatever the Father does the Son also does. For the Father loves the Son and shows him all he does. Yes, to your amazement he will show him even greater things than these. (St. John 5:17, 19–20, NIV)

Recognizing God's authority over His life as well as God's ongoing work in this world, Jesus allowed the Father to remain the determining factor for what He did and how He did it. Because of Jesus' commitment to the Father in that way, the Father in turn revealed Himself—His love, His thoughts, His plans—and gave Jesus the ability to accomplish great things.

That may seem far too spiritual to apply to your career, but I promise you it's not. The beauty of Jesus' life was that He taught us how to live out spiritual principles in the real world. That was one of the primary purposes for His ministry. So, I've taken that to heart.

At each stage in my professional life, I have made it my goal to measure my progress and my transitions by the leading of the Holy Spirit rather than by the prodding of my bosses or the expectations of my well-wishers. In my personal prayer time, I sought the Lord regarding my professional choices, working hard to overcome external pressures to decide or react, even when those factors made *logical* sense to me.

Whenever I have come to God with an openness to hear Him and a willingness to obey, He has given me direction beyond my abilities. He has enabled me to apply for just the right jobs at just the right moments. He has led me to leave companies and cities at the perfect time. He has given me favor and opportunities beyond my imagination, and certainly beyond my ability to plot or plan. Seeking excellence, by allowing God to be my standard bearer, has made all the difference.

But what about that second requirement of excellence—looking inward?

The goal of any athlete competing in a non-team sport is to focus on his **personal best**. He may be aware of his competitors, he may have studied their performances and even made note of their records, but the greatest singular athletes are the ones who overcome *inwardly*. Those who are honest about their skills, maximizing their strengths and focusing intently on the improvement of their weaknesses, will become the strongest competitors.

I'm convinced we have to incorporate that same inward focus into our professional lives. Rather than measure our success by the efforts of our co-workers or the achievements of our chief indus-try rivals, we should come to work each day with an eye toward accomplishing our personal best. How can I utilize my strengths and what steps can I take to improve upon my weaknesses? How can I go to the next level in my knowledge base, my understand-ing, my skill set?

When we approach our work from that vantage point, we don't have to be mean-spirited in our interactions with potential rivals. No one can be the best me, except for me. And because I am confident in my calling and purpose, no one can steal my position or my promotion. We can celebrate the accomplishments of others because they do not pose a threat to us.

In our marketplace, that perspective is so necessary. We spend too many days in senseless comparisons and petty jealousies over the opportunities and accomplishments of others. What if instead we saw the top sales figures of a competitor as good for our entire marketplace? What if we saw mainstream media coverage for one of our Gospel artists as good for the whole genre?

I believe when we are able to work that way, we will be bet-ter as individual professionals, working for stronger companies, serving in a more excellent marketplace.

Final Thoughts

For me, excellence is an ongoing, everyday commitment. It begins with the little things each day—clear communication, follow-through, spell check. It is sometimes tedious and often appears to go unrecognized, but I promise you it's worth it.

The Bible offers wonderful proof of what we've been discuss-ing in the Old Testament. The story of Daniel is, in fact, the most striking example I can offer of the value of excellence.

From childhood, most of us have known about Daniel and the miracle that happened for him inside the den of lions. We are probably less familiar with the consistent commentary on Daniel's character throughout the twelve chapters of the Book of Daniel.

Daniel is said to be a man of great learning, skill, and wisdom who could interpret dreams. More importantly, Daniel is repeatedly said to have possessed an "excellent spirit."[25] In fact, the Bible specifically attributes Daniel's great promotion throughout the land to his personal commitment to excellence:

> *Then this Daniel was preferred above the presidents and princes, because an excellent spirit was in him; and the king thought to set him over the whole realm. (Daniel 6:3, KJV)*

In a foreign land where his people were held as captives, Daniel rose to a position higher than the native leaders. He did it not by plotting to advance himself, or courting the favor of the king. Daniel, instead, gained promotion and great favor through the integrity of his spiritual beliefs and his commitment to develop and maintain excellence.

I believe the example of Daniel is still relevant today.

Those of us called to the Business Community will require favor and wisdom to negotiate our way through the most commercial of systems without losing ourselves, and without compromising our integrity. It is no easy task.

To be truly effective in business and still honor the ministry of Gospel music requires an excellent spirit. I encourage you to make that your goal.

---

[25] Daniel 5:12, Daniel 5:14 (KJV).

Part Four:
Changing Times

A Brief Overview

It would be impossible to complete our discussion without mentioning major shifts that have happened in the overall music industry. If you've watched the news lately or read the key entertainment magazines, you're probably aware of the huge declines in CD sales within the last decade.

After years of watching going-out-of-business sales at independent music stores and hearing the announcements of large-scale store closings by the major music retail chains, those of us who've made our career here are truly beginning to feel the pinch of what I can only call **the death of traditional retail**.

For many years, I have experienced the repeated frustration of walking into a retailer with a "music section" and not finding the CD I had hoped to buy. Even worse, I have had a far more difficult time finding a sales associate with any knowledge of the product I was looking for.

Flash back to the early 1990s: I could hear a brand new song on my local Gospel radio station and within minutes be at the music retailer of my choice buying that CD. Radio heralded the new album, hopefully the radio announcer remembered to confirm the artist and album from which the song came,[26] and I could always count on my favorite sales associate at my favorite local music retailer to know exactly what I was talking about and point me in the right direction. And, in the rare instance that the product was not in stock, they would order it for me without hesitation.

In the summer of 2007, I was the same. I listened for the song, waited for the announcement and headed to store…after store… after store without finding the CD. I was prepared for that from a CD released by a new artist on an independent label. But within the past few years, I have had that increasingly uncomfortable experience for many artists on almost every Gospel label.

How did such a drastic shift happen within the music retail marketplace in such a short period of time?

To fully answer that question, I'd have to bore you with a long list of factors and theories and include a few sales charts with insider terms like YTD, LTD, and TEA. I'd also have to give you a starter course in the digital sales boom and its impact on copyright law. Perhaps someday we will have the opportunity to have that conversation. In the meantime, I'd like to give you a brief—and hopefully simple—look at the changing landscape of Gospel sales in recent years.

In many ways, the Gospel music industry has become a victim of its own success. After decades of being a grassroots, niche market, supported primarily by churchgoers and cultural enthusiasts, Gospel music sales began to increase dramatically about twenty-five years ago.

What appeared first in the 1980s with the multi-platinum success of Christian artists such as Amy Grant and dc Talk, by

---

[26] When a radio announcer names the artist and album for the song he/she just played, we call that "back-announcing" the song.

the early 1990s had begun to spread to core Gospel artists like The Winans, BeBe & CeCe, and Kirk Franklin.

Those successes were driven mainly by increased airplay on mainstream radio stations. But soon the story of gold and platinum success for core Gospel artists drew the attention of mainstream TV news and entertainment media. And with the advent of SoundScan,[27] for the first time within our marketplace there was a way to measure the real financial impact of Gospel music. Attention and investment from major tour promoters soon followed. The Gospel music marketplace grew.

Simultaneously, the overall music industry was rising to unprecedented peaks. In the U.S. alone, music sales hit nearly $15 billion in 1999.[28] Where once the major record companies were satisfied with building their businesses through their various distribution outlets—with great attention to music retailers—this new financial power enabled the major labels to go after higher impact sales at megaretailers.

Ever wonder how it is possible for you to purchase an "exclusive" version of your favorite album from Target or Wal-Mart?

Independent music retailers (also known as Mom & Pop stores) and national music chains (Sam Goody, Coconuts, Tower Records, etc.) tended to purchase music for their stores based upon their knowledge of the marketplace and their relationships with sales executives at the major labels. Music was the majority of their business and they treated it that way, ordering new and catalogue releases, displaying them prominently throughout their

---

[27] SoundScan is a tracking system that monitors the sales of music and video products. It is operated by Nielson Broadcasting, the same company that reports TV ratings.

[28] Rose, Frank "Music Industry Proposes A Piracy Surcharge On ISPs." March 13, 2008. June 19, 2008. *www.wired.com*.

stores and training their in-store staff to service the needs of the dedicated music consumer.

Conversely, for megaretailers like Wal-Mart and Target—brands built upon their diversity of stock—music represents only a small percentage of their overall sales. Their low retail pricing structure is made possible by buying large quantities of items from the manufacturers and spreading them out among their thousands of stores.

Record companies learned that they could create a greater incentive for mass merchants to buy larger quantities of their CDs if they created "exclusive" versions of their new releases. If a fan knew there was a version of their favorite artist's new CD that had an extra song or video and could only be found at Wal-Mart, guess where that fan would be most likely to purchase that CD?

You guessed correctly!

Wal-Mart gets an influx of new customers and the record companies get a greater number of sales through the world's largest retailer. And because Wal-Mart is selling so many copies of the CDs, they can drop the price as well. The megaretailer wins, record companies win, and the consumers win too, right?

Not so fast.

Although that seemed like a phenomenal opportunity for the music industry, the reality is playing out quite differently. There were three major consequences for which the record companies were not adequately prepared:

- The end of the specialty music retailer
- A decrease in music orders from megaretailers
- A lack of exposure for developing artists

The End Of The Specialty Music Retailer

If a consumer could get better versions of a CD at another store, and if that consumer could also get lots of other shopping done at the same time (clothes, electronics, even food), it's not hard to imagine that same consumer would pretty soon stop going to their favorite music retailer altogether.

That's exactly what happened.

Before long, several of the large music chains were facing bankruptcy. They began selling off their inventories and closing their locations. Without the benefits of special versions and lower pricing, the music retailers simply couldn't remain competitive in the marketplace. The independent stores fared even worse.

It is *not* a good thing when the few dedicated outlets for music sales suddenly no longer exist.

I remember stocking up on some catalogue pieces for my CD collection at Tower Records a few years back. To walk in the doors of a store with racks of music as far as my happy, brown eyes could see, and not just one, but two floors. What joy! I had to take an escalator just to *get* to the Gospel music section. And once I was there, I was not disappointed. More than what was current, they stocked what was relevant. They could do that because their music buyers and sales associates understood music.

Recently I went to a megaretailer looking for the new CD from one of my favorite artists, one of the most consistently successful artists in Gospel music—someone with a twenty-year history in the marketplace and platinum sales. It was street week for that artist's newest release and the CD wasn't on the shelf. I ended up going to multiple stores before I could purchase it. And as the sales charts would tell me the following week, it wasn't because all those stores had sold out of their mass quantities. Needless to say, it was a disappointing street week for all concerned.

Suddenly that's the situation for almost any artist. So for people like me, rather than have to stare at a glazey-eyed sales rep who has never even *heard* of the major artists in Gospel music, often my only recourse is to order online or on iTunes.

Now, I love my iPod, but I have to tell you, the album cover alone simply does not do it for me. Credits, people! I must have complete album credits!

Call me old school if you like, but the bottom line is this: There are fewer music specialists in today's retail world and that has proven to be bad most of all for niche music markets like Gospel. Our success has always been measured in more modest numbers than those of our mainstream counterparts. Therefore, lost sales for us are far more painful.

The Impact Of The Megaretailers

After spending so much time and effort to develop a music presence with the megaretailers, the major record labels were certainly not prepared for what happened next. Whether due to an increase in digital sales, file sharing, or a lack of strong product, the exclusives and special versions didn't translate into major increases in profits for megaretailers.

The success of mass retail is based, in large part, on their ability to meticulously track sales and adjust their stock accordingly. So when the numbers for their music sales weren't significant enough, the orders started slowing down.

In fact, if you visit any megaretailer today, you can see evidence of a shift in their music buying philosophy. They tend to stick to the CDs currently charting within the top thirty, and they have decreased the amount of floor space allotted for their music sections. Where Gospel and Christian music are concerned, if a CD does not feature one of the historically top-selling artists, you will have a hard time finding more than one to two units in stock at any given time, if you are fortunate enough to find it at all.

It's important to note that the Wal-Marts, Targets, and Best Buys of the world make far less profit on music sales than on their other merchandise. When most record companies set their wholesale prices for CDs at around $10, a markup to $13.99 doesn't show much of a return. That is why, in the near future, we are likely to see megaretailers pressuring the major labels to drop their wholesale prices. The potential impact of such a move on the quality of albums, the structure of artist and producer contracts, as well as the revenue for all creative personnel is rather scary.

Developing Artists Feel The Pinch

Previously, I mentioned that mass merchants are successful, in large part, by honing their efficiency, keeping track of what is selling where, and adjusting their stock accordingly. Consequently, those locations with a measured history of Gospel CD sales are likely to continue receiving the greatest quantity of new Gospel CDs. Likewise, it is probable that those locations with a history of low or no sales of Gospel CDs will not receive any.

To put this in real terms: When the new Smokie Norful CD comes out, you will have the greatest chance of finding it at the Wal-Mart locations in areas where the customers have a history of buying Smokie's music. You may not find that Smokie Norful CD *at all* in the remaining Wal-Mart locations.

With that in mind, it is easy to understand why the Gospel music presence has become increasingly limited at the megaretailers. Areas where consumers were already inclined to buy Gospel music are often the only areas where Gospel CDs are restocked. Under those circumstances, it becomes difficult to expand consumer awareness into new communities, and even more difficult for new and developing Gospel artists to establish consistent sales.

Truth be told, the developing artist has always had an awkward position in Gospel music. We certainly need new generations of

Gospel artists to ensure a strong marketplace in the future. However, it is *extremely* difficult to break a new artist in Gospel music.

I attribute that fact to one key reason: Despite the number of newer artists at work today, Gospel music remains primarily a vintage marketplace. The majority of the top-selling Gospel artists have been recording for fifteen years or longer.

For proof of that point try this experiment:

Buy a copy of *Billboard* magazine. Make sure it's an issue where the Top Gospel Albums sales chart is printed.[29] Flip to that chart and take a look at those top forty titles. Then count the number of new or developing artists featured on the chart. You are likely to find fewer than 30% of those titles are from new artists.

Now do the same thing with some of the mainstream charts. Flip to the Hot 100, Top R&B Albums, or Top Pop Albums chart and count the number of new artists listed there. You are likely to find a majority of the artists on those charts are new and developing artists, with less than five years of recording history to their credit.

Although challenging from an industry perspective, I don't consider our vintage focus to be something negative. It proves to me that our core consumers—much like consumers of country and blues music—are knowledgeable music lovers who honor the craft of their artists and feel a genuine connection to the history of the music. Their faithfulness enables many of our most talented Gospel artists to become true legends with careers lasting across three decades or more. Artists like Shirley Caesar, The Caravans, Andraé Crouch, Dorothy Norwood, and the Mighty Clouds of Joy have all hit the charts within the past five years. They have all been recording for more than thirty years.

---

[29] The Gospel album sales chart appears in *Billboard* every other week.

It's unlikely we will still see new releases from Rhianna, Lady GaGa, and The Pussycat Dolls even ten years from now.

The downside of being a vintage genre is that it takes a concerted effort to break a new artist in Gospel. Although there are isolated cases of artists who made it to the top of the charts on their first try, for most of Gospel's greats, their first record deal was merely a warm-up. Sometimes it takes as many as four to five albums to firmly establish a Gospel artist with his audience and land him consistently near the top of the charts. This is a long-term marketplace.

With that in mind, the retail crisis has become a real liability for new and developing Gospel artists. In the absence of the dedicated music retailer, there simply isn't time to build an artist's relationship with retail. If you don't come out the gate in the top ten, it becomes very difficult to get significant numbers of CDs into stores.

Unfortunately, Gospel radio exposure is having only a limited impact on this problem. The cold truth is that even if a new artist has a song in heavy rotation at Gospel radio, if the consumer can't find the CD in the store, that airplay is not likely to translate into a sale. And without sales enough for that new artist to remain on the Top Gospel Albums chart, megaretailers probably won't rush to stock more of their CDs.

Now What?

It would be impossible to view the three consequences we've just discussed as small. They are large, and they have more than likely forever changed the way we make and sell music in this country.

In general, most industry people have been aware of the trends we've just discussed for at least the past five years. With the changing landscape at retail and the drastically shifting music-buying habits of consumers, the big record companies have been able to do little more than watch, make predictions, and cut their operating costs.

Unfortunately, big machines find it difficult to innovate when the bulk of their attention must be given to basic questions of survival. It's hard to think about how to break a new artist or take an established artist to a new plateau when you are struggling to figure out simply how to remain profitable.

It is a bleak forecast, but I sincerely believe that all is not lost.

Crisis—particularly financial crisis—tends to breed a certain kind of innovation. We're already beginning to see that trend at work with new forms of Internet outlets for music—legal and illegal—springing up all the time. The legal outlets may help to offset a percentage of the revenue lost from traditional retail.

However, the illegal ones probably tell us more about what music consumers want and how they want it.

Recently, I had an opportunity to give an interview about the future of the music business. I thought long and hard about my answers, and I want to share them with you now.

I honestly believe the overall music industry is moving away from artists as entertainers and music as their method of entertainment. Instead, more and more artists will be purveyors of a lifestyle with music as a vital part of branding that lifestyle.

This change will not be fully realized within the Gospel marketplace for quite some time. Nevertheless, over the next five years, I believe we will see more evidence of what's already happening. People are buying fewer CDs as part of their entertainment mix and more *songs* as accompaniments to their lifestyle. Consequently, Gospel CD sales will continue their downward spiral. Digital sales will increase, but it will not be enough to supplement the loss in CD sales.

In that environment, Gospel artists will have to rethink CD sales as a source of revenue and put more time and attention into discovering and developing a relationship with their audiences through live concerts, direct marketing, and Internet promotions.

Now more than ever, the artist has to know who he is, who his audience is, and what his albums should sound like in light of that audience. The majority of the work to answer those questions is going to be done by the artist and management, not the record labels.

And that's where you come in, my friends. Now more than ever, this marketplace needs fresh faces with new ideas, pure hearts, and an ear toward the Spirit. At this turning point, we need a generation of artists and industry executives who will embrace their profession as calling.

Difficult times call for higher forms of innovation. That's why I'm convinced God is looking for artists as well as industry executives who will not simply rest on their talents and skills, aspiring toward self-promotion. He is looking for those who will be passionate about ministry and excellent in business.

It is a tremendous blessing to know who you are created to be. It is a powerful moment when you realize you were born for this season. It's time to dig in and get to work.

Index

A & R representatives, 45, 80–1, 86, 132, 136, 152
access to markets, record deals and, 104
accessibility, Gospel artists and, 72
advances, artist, 96, 98
agents, booking, 19, 21, 80, 92, 114, 138, 139
aggression, persistence vs., 65–6
albums
    covers of, 47–8
    income from, 95–100
    marketing of, 21, 50, 134–5
    packaging of, 11, 57–9, 134
    production of, 102–3, 132, 151
    promotion of, 21, 50, 101–4, 132–3
    publicity for, 133–4
    sales of, 21, 52, 97–100, 149–50, 158, 177–8
    value to artists of, 150–55
All You Need to Know about the Music Business, 56
all-in producer royalties, 98
American Idol, 91–3
announcers, radio, 133, 136, 177–8
artist agreements, exclusive, 95
artist development, 93
artist management companies, interning with, 147–55
artist's camp, 148
artists, artistry
    accessibility and, 72

artists' aspirations and, 16–7, 35–6
business community and, 13, 20–2, 23–5, 55–62, 114, 125–6, 132, 138, 147–55
business savvy and, 55–62
calling and, 18, 38–9
celebrity and, 17, 35, 54, 64, 71–2, 74–7, 125
church community and, 13, 138
compassion and, 71–4
distinct message and, 42–6, 71
fans and, 71–4, 77, 78–9, 152, 190–1
importance to industry of, 15–6
marketplace changes and, 185–7
patience and, 62–6
persistence and, 65–7
spiritual maturity and, 51–5
success in, 17–8, 37–67
talent and, 17–8, 37–42
unique image and, 46–51
value of music and, 150–55
See also ministry.
audiences, connecting with, 78–9, 190–1
authenticity, importance of, 122–3
auxiliary departments, record company's, 115

Billboard magazine, 145–6, 186
bios, artists', 43, 88

booking agents, 19, 21, 80, 92, 114, 138, 139
brick-and-mortar retailers, 140. *See also* retailers, music.
business affairs departments, 135–6
business community, Gospel music industry's
  biblical model for, 173–4
  breaking into, 114–5, 117–21, 141–56, 158–9
  calling and, 113–6, 117–21
  Church community and, 28–31, 52, 122–3, 138–9
  commitment to excellence and, 157–160
  comparative excellence in, 169–73
  compassion for artists and, 120, 124–6
  components of, 19–25, 114, 141
  creative community and, 13, 20–2, 23–5, 55–62, 114, 125–6, 132, 138, 147–55
  Daniel as model for, 173–4
  excellence in, 157–74
  job titles in, 166–9
  jobs in, 158–9
  limited information about, 11–12, 20
  roles within, 131–40
  servanthood and, 120, 126–9, 160
  skill-set for, 160–6
  source books for, 59–60
  spiritual foundation and, 120–4
  trade magazines for, 145–7
  See also record companies.
business managers, 137
business savvy, acquiring, 55–62

calling
  artistry and, 35–6, 38–9, 52–3, 66
  God's long-term goals and, 3–6, 18, 31, 39, 117–21
  industry and, 113–6, 117–21
catalogues, record company, 170
celebrity, 17, 35, 54, 64, 71–2, 74–7, 125
CD packaging, 57–9

CDs
  covers of, 47–8
  income from, 95–100
  marketing of, 21, 50, 134–5
  packaging of, 11, 57–9, 134
  production of, 102–3, 132, 151
  promotion of, 21, 50, 101–4, 132–3
  publicity for, 133–4
  sales of, 21, 52, 97–100, 149–50, 158, 177–8
  value to artists of, 150–55
character, development of, 63–5, 73–4, 126, 129
Christian entertainment, ministry vs., 54–5
Christian/Gospel Industry Directory, GMA's, 59–60
Christianity, artists' relationship to, 18, 28, 30. *See also* faith, foundation of *and related topics.*
Church Community
  business community and, 28–31, 52, 122–3, 138–9
  connecting with culture of, 122–3
  creative community and, 122–3, 138
  place in Gospel music industry of, 18, 27–31, 52, 105
  promoters and, 139
Commissioned, 47–9
communication skills, 163–6
comparative excellence, 169–73
compassion, developing, 71–4, 124–6
competitiveness
  of Gospel music industry, 157–9, 170
  value to artists of, 41–2
concert promoters, 21, 80, 139–40
conferences, attending, 42, 108–9, 142–5
confidence, built on God, 67
contracts. *See* record deals.
contractual language, 96
creative community, Gospel music's
  accessibility and, 72
  artists' aspirations and, 16–7, 35–6

business community and, 13, 20–2, 23–5, 55–62, 114, 125–6, 132, 138, 147–55
business savvy and, 55–62
calling and, 18, 38–9
celebrity and, 17, 35, 54, 64, 71–2, 74–7, 125
church community and, 13, 122–3, 138
compassion and, 71–4
distinct message and, 42–6, 71
fans and, 71–4, 77, 78–9, 152, 190–1
importance to industry of, 15–6
marketplace changes and, 185–7
patience and, 62–6
persistence and, 65–7
spiritual maturity and, 51–5
success in, 17–8, 37–67
talent and, 17–8, 37–42
unique image and, 46–51
value of music and, 150–55
See also ministry.
credibility, record deals and, 103–4
cross-collateralization, 98

Daniel, excellence modeled by, 173–4
demo policies, record companies', 88–9
demos
promoting, 60
creating, 66, 80–90
detail, attention to, 163–6
determination, value of, 65–7
developing artists
in new music marketplace, 185–7
working with labels and, 108, 118, 132
See also creative community.
digital music outlets, 140, 178, 182, 189–90
distinct message, artists', 42–6, 71

entertainment lawyers, 98, 109, 135–6
"entourage disease," 158
entry-level positions, obtaining, 114–5, 117–21, 142, 147–55

excellence, commitment to, 157–74
exclusive artist agreements, 95

faith, foundation of, 22, 30–1, 79, 121–4, 160
fame, 17, 35, 54, 64, 71–2, 74–7, 125
fans, relating to, 71–4, 77, 78–9, 152
follow-up, skill of, 163–6
Foth, Richard, 116
funding, record deals and, 102–3

gifts, individual, 3–6, 18
GMA's *Christian/Gospel Industry Directory*, 59–60
Gordy, Berry, 92–3
Gospel Announcers Guild (GAG), 137
Gospel, communicating the, 51–5, 71, 104. *See also* ministry.
Gospel Music Association, 59–60, 145
Gospel music industry
business community and, 11–3, 19–25. *See also separate entry.*
church community and, 13, 27–31. *See also separate entry.*
competitiveness of, 157–9
creative community of, and, 15–8. *See also separate entry.*
future of, 189–91
knowledge of, 141–55
source books for, 59–60
trends in, 25, 93–4, 108, 177–187, 189–91
vintage character of, 186–7
See also mainstream music industry, record companies *and* record deals.
Gospel Music Industry Round-Up, The, 59
Gospel music marketplace, 96
Gospel Music Workshop of America (GMWA), 137, 145
growth plan, spiritual, 63–5

Hammond, Fred, 12, 49, 119–20
head shots, 88
Holy Spirit, character and, 73–4

hope, from experience, 63–4, 71
humility, 75–8, 121, 127–8
hype, truth vs., 157–9

illegal downloading sites, 189–90
image, artists', 20, 31, 46–51
income. *See* royalties.
independent music retailers, decline of, 179–82
industry. *See* business community, Gospel music industry's.
industry source books, 59–60
industry trade magazines, 145–7
innovation, in Gospel music, 189–91
inspiration for music, 28
in-studio performance skills, 82–3, 105
Internet marketing, 134
Internet sales outlets, 140, 178, 182, 189–90
internships
    at record labels, 60–2
inward focus, professional life and, 172–3

Jesus Christ
    compassion of, 73–4
    conduct of professional life and, 171–2
    servanthood of, 75–7
job titles, pursuit of, 166

labels. *See* record companies.
lawyers, entertainment, 98, 109, 135–6
legal departments, 135–6
lifestyle, Christian artists', 28, 30–1, 190
live performances, 19, 52, 78–9, 81–4, 139
live recordings, 78–9, 81–3
local churches
    artists' relationship with, 18, 27, 37–8, 54, 105
    live performances in, 79
    promoters and, 139
    See also Church Community.
local vs. national artists, 38–42

lyrics, song, 58, 71

mainstream music industry, 13, 27, 42–3, 46, 47, 53, 57, 71, 74–5, 92–4, 100, 177–9
mainstream music marketplace, 96, 177–80
management companies, artist, 147–55
management teams, artists', 19, 20, 137–9
marketing, 20–1, 43, 50, 134–5, 136
    jobs in, 134–5
    See also promotions *and* publicity.
maturity, spiritual, 51–5
media
    jobs in, 137
    promotions and, 19, 20, 29, 104
megaretailers, music marketplace and, 179–80, 182–4
message, distinct, 42–6, 71
message, Gospel music's, 42–3
ministry
    Christian entertainment vs., 54–5
    developing, 18, 36, 44, 46, 52, 64, 66, 69–70, 73–8, 90, 101–2, 104–7
    record company choice and, 108–9
    record deals and, 104–7, 109
moment of first risk, 152–3
Motown Records, 92–3
multiple income streams, 99
musical styles, demos and, 85
musicals, 79

name-dropping, 159
national vs. regional artists, 38–42
networking, 118–9, 144
new artist showcases, 79

objectitivity, value of, 61
on-line music outlets, 140
open-mic nights, 42, 79
oral communication skills, 163–6
outward achievement, distraction by, 166–9
overdubs, 82

overnight success, 63–4

packaging
    CD, 11, 57–9, 134
    demos and, 88
packaging deductions, 98
Passman, Donald S., 56
patience, value of, 62–5
perfectionism, 159
performance, measuring, 169–73
persistence, value of, 65–7
personal best, professional life and,
    172–3
personal managers, 137
personal relationships, 72–4, 165–6
prayer life, importance of, 74, 78, 124
press kits, 21, 22
press releases, 21, 22
primary forums, Gospel artists', 28
producer royalties, 96, 98, 99
producers, 15, 96, 98, 99
production costs, CDs, 102–3
production quality, demos and, 85–7
production skills, 99–100
production styles, demos and, 85
professional life, in industry, 169–73
programming directors, radio, 133, 136
promoters, concert, 21, 80, 139–40
promotion, humility and, 127–8
promotions, 19, 20, 21, 29, 43, 104,
    132–3, 136–7, 177, 179, 187. *See also*
    marketing *and* publicity.
ProTools software, 87
public performances. *See* live
    performances.
public relations programs, 22–3
publicists, 133–4
publicity, jobs in, 133–4. *See also*
    marketing *and* promotions.

radio, jobs in, 136–7
radio announcers, 133, 136, 177–8
radio promotions, 19, 20, 21, 29, 43,
    104, 132–3, 136–7, 177, 179, 187
reality TV contests, 16–7, 91–2, 93–4

record companies
    auxiliary departments of, 115–6
    CD promotion and, 101–4
    choice of, 107–9
    church communities and, 28–9
    demos and, 80–90
    interning for, 60–2
    jobs in, 131–6
    market changes and, 179–87
    record deals and, 91–109
    role in industry of, 19–21
    roles in, 131–6
    scarcity of, 86
    structure of, 115
record deals
    access to markets and, 104
    advantages of, 100–4
    basic structure of, 94–100
    credibility and, 103–4
    difficulty of landing, 86
    funding and, 102–3
    history of, 92–4
    legal departments and, 135–6
    ministry and, 101–2, 104–7
    pros and cons of, 104–7
    realities of, 91–4
record labels. *See* record companies.
recording budgets, 96
recording contracts. *See* record deals.
recording studios, creating demos in, 87
recoupable advances, 98
recoupable marketing costs, 98
recoupment, 96–8
regional vs. national artists, 38–42
rehearsals, 78
retailers, music
    CD sales and, 104, 134–5, 149–50,
        177–84
    decline of traditional, 177–91
    independent, 179–82
    Internet, 140, 178, 182, 189–90
    jobs in, 140
    on-line, 140
    role in industry of, 19, 21, 114
    speciality, 181–2

risk, moment of first, 152–3
road managers, 137–8
royalties
    artists', 96–9
    producers', 96, 98, 99

sales departments, record company, 21,
    134, 135
sales outlets. *See* retailers, music.
savvy, business, 55–62
servanthood, 74–8, 117–8, 124, 126–9,
    160
showcases for music, 28
showmanship, 53–4
singers, creating demos and, 83–4
singles, album, 21, 29, 43
skill-set, for industry professionals,
    160–6
Solomon, humility and, 127
song choices, demos and, 83–4
song lyrics, 58, 71
songwriters, 15, 83–4, 99, 151
songwriting skills, 99–100
SoundScan, 179
source books, industry, 59–60
sources of talent, 28
specialty music retailers, decline of,
    181–2
spin, truth vs., 157–9
spiritual development, industry
    professionals and, 121–4
spiritual foundation, industry
    professionals and, 120–4
spiritual growth plans, 63–5

spiritual maturity, artists', 51–5
"street week," CD's, 150, 182
studio performance skills, 82–3, 105
styling teams, 50
success, real vs. apparent, 158–9, 167–9
support team, artist's, 138

talent competitions, 42
talent, individual
    calling vs., 3–6
    importance of, 17–8, 38
    sources of, 28
    world-class, 38–42
"thank yous," CD liner notes and, 58
titles, job, 166–9
tools, gifts and talents and, 3–6
tours, promoters and, 139
trade magazines, industry, 145–7

unique image, artists', 46–51
unpaid internships, 62
unpaid publicity, 134
unrecouped earnings, 97
unsolicited demos, 89

vintage focus, industry's, 186–7
volunteerism, 70

Walmart, retail sales and, 179–80
"work for hire," 55
workplace relationships, 165–6
workshops, attending, 42
world-class talent, 38–42
written communication skills, 163–6

ORDER FORM

Fax orders: (866) 899-6419. Send this form.

Email orders: send the information requested on this form to pmpublishing@monicacoates.com

On-line orders: Please visit *www.monicacoates.com*

Postal orders: send this form to Paul Marchell Publishing P.O. Box 682854, Franklin, TN 37068, USA

Please send _____ copies of *The Beginner's Guide To The Gospel Music Industry* ($16.95 each + shipping as outlined below)

Name: _____

Address Line 1: _____

Address Line 2: _____

City: _____ State: _____ Zip: _____

Telephone: _____

Email: _____

Sales Tax: Please add 9.25% sales tax for products shipped to Tennessee addresses.

Shipping

U.S.: $3.00 for first book and $2.00 for each additional book.

International: $9.00 (USD) for first book and $5.00 (USD) for each additional book (estimate).

PAUL MARCHELL
PUBLISHING

ORDER FORM

Fax orders: (866) 899-6419. Send this form.

Email orders: send the information requested on this form to pmpublishing@monicacoates.com

On-line orders: Please visit *www.monicacoates.com*

Postal orders: send this form to Paul Marchell Publishing P.O. Box 682854, Franklin, TN 37068, USA

Please send _____ copies of *The Beginner's Guide To The Gospel Music Industry* ($16.95 each + shipping as outlined below)

Name: _____

Address Line 1: _____

Address Line 2: _____

City: _____ State: _____ Zip: _____

Telephone: _____

Email: _____

Sales Tax: Please add 9.25% sales tax for products shipped to Tennessee addresses.

Shipping

U.S.: $3.00 for first book and $2.00 for each additional book.

International: $9.00 (USD) for first book and $5.00 (USD) for each additional book (estimate).

PAUL MARCHELL
PUBLISHING

About the Author

Photo by Mark Luckey

MONICA COATES is a veteran of the Gospel music industry with experience in artist management, publicity, radio promotions, and A&R. Over the course of a diverse career, she has worked at the top Gospel labels—EMI Gospel and Verity—and with a variety of artists, including Fred Hammond, Donnie McClurkin, Hezekiah Walker, and Joann Rosario.

After earning a Bachelor of Arts degree in English and Afro-American Studies from the University of Virginia and a Master of Arts degree in Journalism from the University of Maryland at College Park, Monica was set to pursue a career as a journalist. In the fall of 1991, she felt a call to turn her attentions instead toward service in the Gospel music industry, where she has made her livelihood since 1992.

Monica currently resides near Nashville, TN. She serves as a speaker and music industry consultant.

Breinigsville, PA USA
07 December 2009
228753BV00001B/29/P